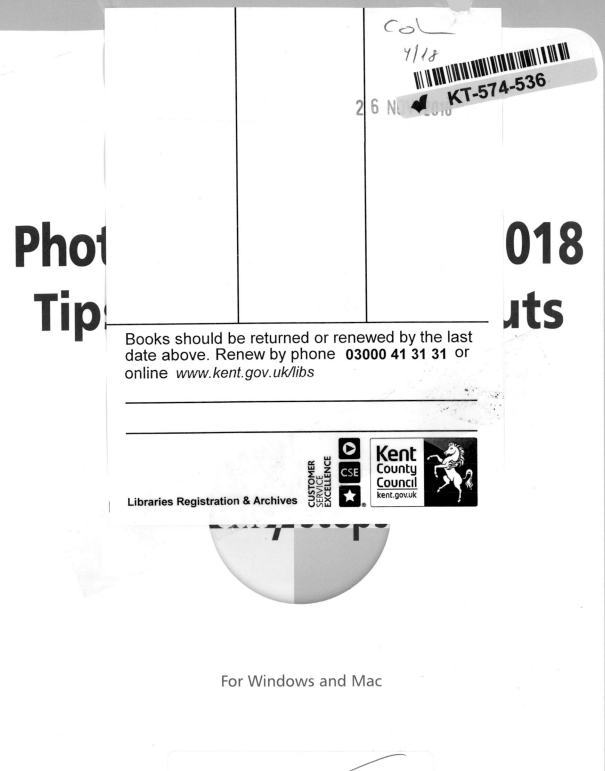

Phot

Tips

018

uts

For Windows and Mac

In easy steps is an imprint of In Easy Steps Limited
16 Hamilton Terrace · Holly Walk · Leamington Spa
Warwickshire · United Kingdom · CV32 4LY
www.ineasysteps.com

Notice of Liability
Every effort has been made to ensure that this book contains accurate
and current information. However, In Easy Steps Limited and the
author shall not be liable for any loss or damage suffered by readers
as a result of any information contained herein.

Trademarks
Photoshop® is a registered trademark of Adobe Systems Incorporated.
All other trademarks are acknowledged as belonging to their
respective companies.

In Easy Steps Limited supports The Forest Stewardship Council (FSC),
the leading international forest certification organization. All our titles
that are printed on Greenpeace approved FSC certified paper carry the
FSC logo.

MIX
Paper from
responsible sources
FSC® C020837

Printed and bound in the United Kingdom

ISBN 978-1-84078-803-7

Contents

1 Introducing Elements

Photoshop Elements is a digital image-editing program that comprehensively spans the gap between very basic programs and professional-level ones. This chapter introduces the various workspaces and modes of Elements, shows how to access them, and details what can be done with each one.

About Elements

Photoshop Elements is the offspring of the professional-level image-editing program, Photoshop. Photoshop is somewhat unusual in the world of computer software, in that it is widely accepted as being the best program of its type on the market. If professional designers or photographers are using an image-editing program, it will almost certainly be Photoshop. However, two of the potential drawbacks to Photoshop are its cost and its complexity. This is where Elements comes into its own. Adobe (the maker of Photoshop and Elements) has recognized that the majority of digital imaging users (i.e. the consumer market) want something with the basic power of Photoshop, but with enough user-friendly features to make it easy to use, and for a reasonable price. With the explosion in the digital camera market, a product was needed to meet the needs of a new generation of image editors – and that product is Photoshop Elements.

Elements contains most of the same powerful editing/color management tools as the full version of Photoshop, and it also includes a number of versatile features for sharing images and for creating artistic projects, such as slideshows, cards, calendars and cover photos for Facebook. It also has valuable features, such as the Guided edit and Quick edit modes, where you can quickly apply editing techniques and follow step-by-step processes to achieve a range of creative and artistic effects.

Special effects

One of the great things about using Elements with digital images is that it provides numerous fun and creative options for turning mediocre images into eye-catching works of art. This is achieved through a wide variety of step-by-step activities within Guided edit mode, which have been added to and enhanced in Elements 2018.

Advanced features

In addition to user-friendly features, Elements also has an Expert edit mode where you can use a range of advanced features, including a full set of tools for editing and color adjustments.

Photoshop Elements can be bought online directly from Adobe, as well as from other computer and software sites, or at computer software stores. There are Windows and Mac versions of the program, and with Elements 2018 these are virtually identical. If Elements 2018 is bought from the Adobe website, at **www.adobe.com**, it can be downloaded and installed directly from there. Otherwise it will be provided on a DVD, with a serial number that needs to be entered during installation.

The New icon pictured above indicates a new or enhanced feature introduced with the latest version – Photoshop Elements 2018 (also referred to as Photoshop Elements 18).

Welcome Screen

When you first open Elements, you will be presented with the Welcome Screen. This offers initial advice about working with Elements and also provides options for accessing the different workspaces. The Welcome Screen appears by default, but this can be altered once you become more familiar with Elements.

Welcome Screen functions

 1 Options for organizing photos, editing them and using them in a variety of creative ways

 2 Click on the **Organizer** button to go to that area

 3 Click on the **Photo Editor** button to go to that area

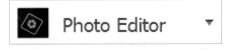

The Welcome Screen can be accessed at any time by selecting **Help** > **Welcome Screen** from the Photo Editor or Organizer Menu bar. Click on this button at the top of the Welcome Screen to select options for what happens when Elements is launched.

The **Video Editor** button on the Welcome Screen links to Adobe Premiere Elements (sold separately), which is the video editing companion app to Photoshop Elements.

9

Don't forget

In Elements 2018 there is also an **eLive** button on the top toolbar. This links to a range of help and news articles about Elements.

Don't forget

The Elements Organizer can be accessed from any of the Editor modes by clicking on the Organizer button on the Taskbar.

Hot tip

The keyboard shortcut for closing Elements is Ctrl + Q (Command key + Q on a Mac).

Photo Editor Workspace

From the Welcome Screen, the Photo Editor workspace can be accessed. This is a combination of the work area (where images are opened and edited), menus, toolbars, toolboxes and panels. At first it can seem a little daunting, but Elements has been designed with three different editing modes to give you as many options as possible for editing your photos.

The components of the Photo Editor (Editor) are:

Menu bar   Editor mode buttons   Panel bin

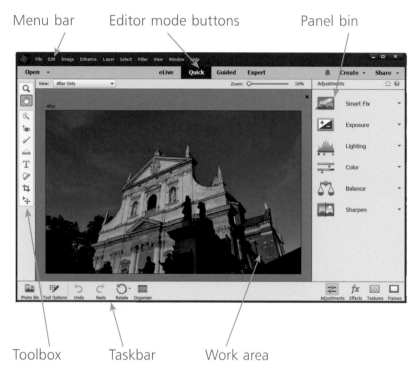

Toolbox   Taskbar   Work area

Editor modes

The three different modes in the Photo Editor are accessed from the buttons at the top of the Elements window. They are:

- **Quick edit mode**. This can be used to perform quick editing options in one step.

- **Guided edit mode**. This can be used to perform a range of editing techniques, following a step-by-step process for each.

- **Expert edit mode**. This can be used for ultimate control over the editing process.

...cont'd

Taskbar and Tool Options

The Taskbar is the group of buttons that is available across all three Editor modes, at the bottom left of the Elements window:

One of the options on the Taskbar is Tool Options. This displays the available options for any tool selected from the Toolbox (different tools are available in each of the different Editor modes). See pages 18-19 for details.

Photo Bin

The Photo Bin is another feature that can be accessed from all three Editor modes. The Photo Bin enables you to quickly access all of the images that you have open within the Editor. To use the Photo Bin:

 Open two or more images. The most recently-opened one will be the one that is active in the Editor window

 All open images are shown here in the Photo Bin

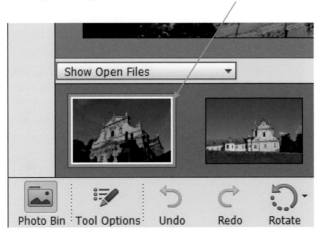

3. Click on an image in the Photo Bin to make that the active one for editing

The items on the Taskbar are, from left to right: show or hide the Photo Bin, show or hide the Tool Options bar, Undo the previous actions, Redo any undone actions, Rotate the active photo, and access the Organizer. In Expert edit mode there is also an option to change the Layout.

Images can also be made active for editing by dragging them directly from the Photo Bin and dropping them within the Editor window.

When image editing has begun, this icon appears at its top right-hand corner in the Photo Bin.

11

Quick Edit Mode

Quick edit mode contains a number of functions that can be selected from panels and applied to an image, without the need to manually apply all of the commands. To do this:

 In the Editor, click on the **Quick** button

For a more detailed look at Quick edit mode, see pages 82-87.

 The currently-active image is displayed within the Quick edit window. This has the standard Taskbar and Photo Bin, and a reduced Toolbox. Click here to access the Quick edit panels

Some of the options in the Adjustments panel in Quick edit mode (Step 3) have an Auto option for applying the effect in a single click.

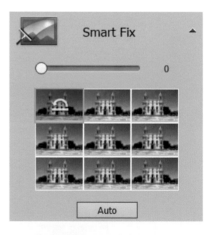 Select one of the commands to have it applied to the active image. This can be applied either by clicking on one of the thumbnail options or by dragging the appropriate slider at the top of the panel

Move the cursor over one of the thumbnails to view a real-time preview of the effect on the open image. Click on one of the thumbnails to apply the effect.

 Click on these buttons on the Taskbar at the bottom of the Quick edit panel to select **Adjustments**, **Effects**, **Textures** and **Frames** options for adding to photos

Guided Edit Mode

Guided edit mode focuses on common tasks for editing digital images, and shows you how to perform them with a step-by-step process. To use Guided edit mode:

 1 In the Editor, click on the **Guided** button

Some new effects have been added to Guided edits in Elements 2018.

2 The Guided edit window contains a range of categories that can be accessed from buttons at the top of the window. Each category contains Guided edit options. Drag the mouse over each item to view the before and after effect

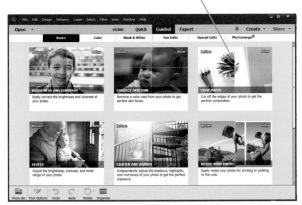

Don't forget

Guided edit mode is a great place to start if you are new to image editing, or feel unsure about anything to do with it.

13

3 Each item has its own wizard to perform the required task. This will take you through a step-by-step process for undertaking the selected action. Move through the steps to complete the selected Guided edit option

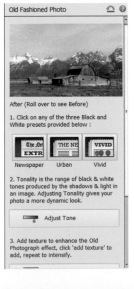

Old Fashioned Photo

After (Roll over to see Before)

1. Click on any of the three Black and White presets provided below :

Newspaper   Urban   Vivid

2. Tonality is the range of black & white tones produced by the shadows & light in an image. Adjusting Tonality gives your photo a more dynamic look.

Adjust Tone

3. Add texture to enhance the Old Photograph effect, click 'add texture' to add, repeat to intensify.

Don't forget

Different Guided edits have varying numbers of steps in the required wizards, but the process is similar for all of them.

Expert Edit Mode

Expert edit mode is where you can take full editing control over your photos. It has a range of powerful editing tools so that you can produce subtle and impressive effects. To use Expert edit mode:

Select **Window** > **Tools** from the Menu bar to show or hide the Toolbox.

1 In the Editor, click on the **Expert** button

Expert

2 The full range of editing tools is available:

Expert edit mode Toolbox   Open panels

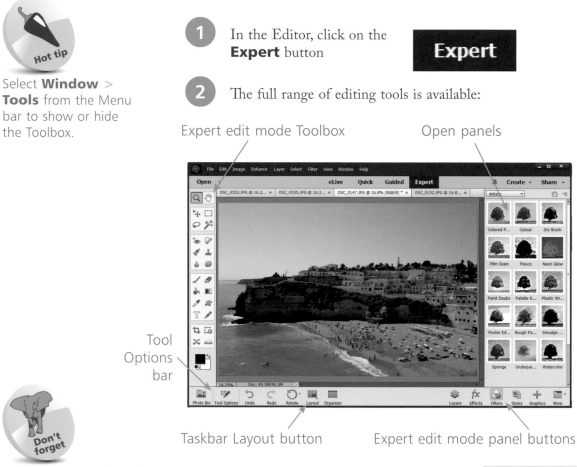

Tool Options bar

Taskbar Layout button   Expert edit mode panel buttons

When a tool is selected in the Toolbox, the Tool Options bar (above the Taskbar) has various options for the selected tool; see pages 18-19.

The **Layout** button is the one addition on the Taskbar within Expert edit mode, as opposed to Quick and Guided edit modes. Click on the **Layout** button to access options for the display of your open photos within the Editor window.

Column and Rows

Rows and Column

All Grid

All Column

All Row

All Floating

Default

Layout   Organizer

14

...cont'd

The Expert edit mode Toolbox

The Toolbox in Expert edit mode contains tools for applying a wide range of editing techniques. Some of the tools have more than one option. To see if a tool has additional options:

1 Move the cursor over the **Toolbox**. Tools that have additional options appear with a small arrow in the top right-hand corner of their icons. Click on a tool to view the options within the Tool Options bar

The default Toolbox tools are (keyboard shortcut in brackets):

Don't forget

The tools that have additional options are: Crop, Marquee, Lasso, Quick Selection, Spot Healing Brush, Type, Smart Brush, Eraser, Brush, Clone Stamp, Custom Shape, Blur, and Sponge.

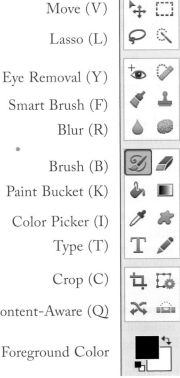

Zoom (Z)	Hand (H)
Move (V)	Rectangular Marquee (M)
Lasso (L)	Quick Selection (A)
Red Eye Removal (Y)	Spot Healing Brush (J)
Smart Brush (F)	Clone Stamp (S)
Blur (R)	Sponge (O)
Brush (B)	Eraser (E)
Paint Bucket (K)	Gradient (G)
Color Picker (I)	Custom Shape (U)
Type (T)	Pencil (N)
Crop (C)	Recompose (W)
Content-Aware (Q)	Straighten (K)
Foreground Color	Background Color

Hot tip

Keyboard shortcuts can be used by pressing the Shift key and the appropriate letter.

Hot tip

Hold down the Alt key and click on the tools in the Toolbox to scroll through the additional options, if available.

Tool Options Bar

When a tool is selected from the Toolbox, in either Expert or Quick mode, the Tool Options bar is activated on the Taskbar. This provides options for selecting different tools from that category (if there are any), and also settings for the currently selected tool. To use the Tool Options bar:

1 Select a tool from the Toolbox

2 Click here on the Taskbar to hide or show the Tool Options bar

3 The Tool Options bar is positioned above the Taskbar at the bottom of the Elements window

4 Click here to select different tools from the selected category (in this example it is the Brush tool, the Impressionist Brush tool or the Color Replacement tool)

5 For each item there are different settings available; e.g. for the Brush tool there is **Brush** type, **Size** and **Opacity** (how much of the background is visible through the selected brush stroke). There are also options for a wider Brush range, including **Mode** and **Brush Settings...**

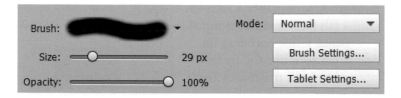

Don't forget

Use these buttons in the top right-hand corner of the Tool Options bar to, from left to right: access the Help options for the selected tool; access the Tool Options menu; or hide the Tool Options bar (click on a tool to display the Tool Options bar again).

Hot tip

Brush **Mode** has several options for how the brush stroke interacts with the background behind it; e.g. Color Burn, Lighten or Soft Light. These can be used to create artistic effects with the Brush tool and the photo itself.

Don't forget

For a more detailed look at Brush style settings, see pages 160-161.

6 Other tools have different settings available from the Tool Options bar. For instance, the **Zoom** tool has options for zooming the currently active image to different magnifications, and also viewing it at specific sizes; e.g. **1:1**, **Fit Screen**, **Fill Screen** and **Print Size**

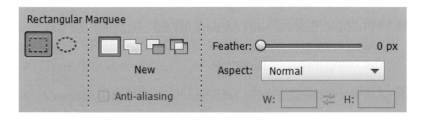

7 The **Type** tool has options for font type, font style, font color, font size, leading (the space between lines of text), bold, italics, underline, strikethrough and also text alignment (left, center or right)

The Type tool also has options for changing the orientation of text and also Text Warp for special effects; see page 148 for details.

8 For the **Marquee** tool and the **Lasso** tool there are options for editing a current selection (add to selection, subtract from selection and intersect with selection) and also for the amount of Feathering to be applied. This determines how much around the edge of the selection is slightly blurred, to give a soft-focus effect. The Marquee tool also has an option for setting a specific aspect for the selection; i.e. create it at a fixed ratio or size

The Marquee and Lasso tools are used to make selections by dragging the tool over the image. This can be symmetrical selections, e.g. Rectangular Marquee, or freehand, e.g. Lasso.

Organizer Workspace

The Organizer workspace contains functions for sorting, viewing and finding multiple images. To use the Organizer:

 In any of the Editor modes, click on the **Organizer** button on the Taskbar

The Organizer has four views, in addition to eLive (see page 10), accessed from these buttons:

- Media View **Media**
- People View **People**
- Places View **Places**
- Events View **Events**

Media View

The Media View displays thumbnails of your photos, and also has functions for sorting and finding images:

Folders and Albums   View buttons   Thumbnails

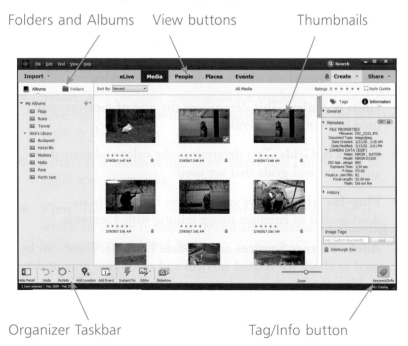

Organizer Taskbar   Tag/Info button

Editor

Click on these buttons to apply image-editing effects to a selected image in Media View, or view the Tags and Information panels

For information about using tags and keywords, see pages 46-47.

People View

This view can be used to tag specific people and then view photos with those people in them.

For information about using the Organizer, and its different views, see Chapter 2.

Places View

This view can be used to place photos on a map so that they can be searched for by location.

When you have a group of photos from the same location, add them to Places View so that this can be used to search over your photos.

Events View

This view can be used to group photos according to specific events such as birthdays and vacations.

Create Mode

Create mode is where you can release your artistic flair and start designing items such as photo books and photo collages. It can also be used to create slideshows, and to put your images onto discs. To use Create mode:

Use the Facebook Cover option to create a photo montage that is sized at the correct size to be used as your Facebook cover photo.

24

Use your 12 best photos when using the Photo Calendar option.

Create mode projects take longer than normal image-editing functions.

1 In either the Editor or the Organizer, click on the **Create** button

Create ▾

2 Select one of the Create projects. Each project has a wizard that takes you through the Create process. The projects include Photo Books, Greeting Cards, Photo Calendars, Photo Collages, cover photos for Facebook and covers for CDs/DVDs

Slideshow
Photo Prints
Photo Book
Greeting Card
Photo Calendar
Photo Collage
Instant Movie
Video Story
Video Collage
DVD with Menu
Facebook Cover
CD Jacket
DVD Jacket
CD/DVD Label

3 The Create wizard takes you through the process so you can display your photos in a variety of creative ways

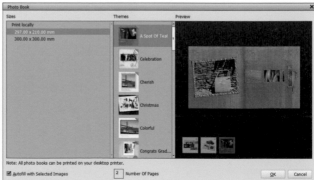

4 For most creations there is a theme that can be applied, to which your own photos can then be added

Click on the **Print** button once a creation has been made, to produce a hard copy.

Print

5 Your photos can be added automatically from the Photo Bin, or you can drag them directly from there onto the creation

Click on the **Save** button to save a completed creation in a specific file format, and the **Close** button to exit Create mode without saving the project.

Save   Close

6 Once your photos have been added, a new file is created, to which you can add text, layout designs and graphics. Click on any available text boxes to add text there, click on the **Layouts** button to change the layout of the creation, and click on the **Graphics** button to add a background

7 Click on the **Advanced Mode** button to access the Expert mode Toolbox, which can be used to edit the creation in the same way as for a standard photo

Advanced Mode

Share Mode

Share mode can be used to distribute your images to family and friends in a number of creative ways. To use Share mode:

 In the Organizer, click on the **Share** button

 Select one of the Share options, such as sharing to social media sites, sharing via email or creating a DVD or PDF slideshow

Beware

The Share function can also be accessed from within the Editor, but there are fewer share options available.

 If you are sharing to email, the selected item is added to a wizard that can be used to determine the size and quality of the attachment that you want to send. Click on the **Next** button to move through the wizard

Beware

To share an image in an email you need to have an appropriate email app on your computer, and an internet connection.

4 For sharing to social media sites, such as Facebook, Flickr and Twitter, Elements

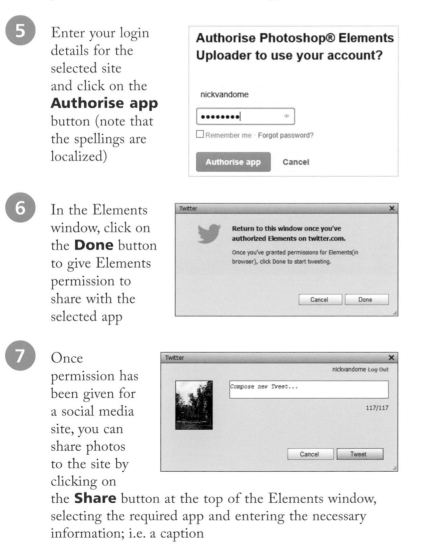

has to initially be authorized to share content to these sites. Click on the **Authorize** button to give Elements permission to share to the selected app

5 Enter your login details for the selected site and click on the **Authorise app** button (note that the spellings are localized)

6 In the Elements window, click on the **Done** button to give Elements permission to share with the selected app

7 Once permission has been given for a social media site, you can share photos to the site by clicking on

the **Share** button at the top of the Elements window, selecting the required app and entering the necessary information; i.e. a caption

There is always some risk in giving websites authorization to access your computer.

You must already have an account with a specific social media site in order to authorize Elements to use it; you cannot create an account during this process.

You only have to authorize Elements to use a social media site once. After that, photos can be shared in two clicks from the **Share** menu.

27

Getting Help

One of the differences between Elements and the full version of Photoshop is the amount of assistance and guidance offered by each program. Since Photoshop is aimed more at the professional end of the market, the level of help is confined largely to the standard help directory, which serves as an online manual. Elements also contains this, but in addition it has the Getting Started option, which is designed to take users through the digital image-editing process as smoothly as possible. The Getting Started option offers general guidance about digital imaging techniques and there are also help items that can be accessed by selecting Help from the Menu bar. These include online help; information on available plug-ins for Elements; tutorials; and support details.

Using the help files

eLive is a function in Elements 2018 that provides a selection of tutorials and videos for getting the most out of Elements. To access these, click on the **eLive** button on the top toolbar in either Editor or Organizer mode.

eLive

1 Select **Photoshop Elements Help** from the **Help** menu and click on an item to display it in the main window. Click on the links at the left-hand side to navigate through each section

The keyboard shortcut for Photoshop Elements Help is F1.

A Adobe   Creativity & Design   Marketing & Analytics   PDF & E-Signatures   Business Solutions   Support   🔍   Sign In

PHOTOSHOP ELEMENTS   Learn & Support   User Guide   Tutorials

Photoshop Elements User Guide

Search Adobe Support   🔍

📑 TOPICS

Introduction to Photoshop Elements	>
Workspace and environment	>
Fixing and enhancing photos	>
Adding shapes and text	>
Guided edits, effects, and filters	>
Working with colors	>
Working with selections	>

INTRODUCTION TO PHOTOSHOP ELEMENTS

Welcome to the Adobe Photoshop Elements User Guide! Choose a topic from the left to find answers, get step-by-step instructions, and develop your skills.

Not what you're looking for? Go back to Photoshop Elements Learn & Support for more resources.

Photoshop Elements 2018 Overview
Use Photoshop Elements to

What's new in Photoshop Elements
Find out what's new in

2 Organizing Images

This chapter shows how to download digital images via Elements and how to view and organize them, including using the People, Places, and Events views. It shows how you can tag images so that they are easy to find, how to search for items according to a variety of criteria, and how to use albums and folders to organize and manage images.

Obtaining Images

One of the first tasks in Elements is to import images so that you can start editing and sharing them. This can be done from a variety of devices, but the process is similar for all of them. To import images into Elements:

 Access the **Organizer** by clicking on this button in the Editor

Organizer

 Select **File** > **Get Photos and Videos** from the Menu bar and select the type of device from which you want to load images into Elements, or

From Files and Folders...	Ctrl+Shift+G
From Camera or Card Reader...	Ctrl+G
From Scanner...	Ctrl+U
In Bulk...	

 Click on the **Import** button and select one of the options for obtaining images

Import ▾	
	From Files and Folders...
	From Camera or Card Reader...
	From Scanner...
	In Bulk...

4 If you select **From Camera or Card Reader...,** click the drop-down arrow beside **Get Photos from:** to select a specific device. This can include directly from a digital camera (connected to your computer with a USB cable), a smartphone or a memory card, using a memory card reader

Get Photos from:

Apple iPhone	⌄
Apple iPhone	
E:\<Camera or Card Reader>	
< Refresh List >	

5 The number of files selected to be downloaded are shown under the **Get Photos from:** drop-down box in the Photo Downloader window

6 Click the **Browse...** button to select a destination for the selected images

Elements Organizer - Photo Downloader ✕

Source

Get Photos from:
E:\<Camera or Card Reader> ⌄
1293 Files Selected - 7.3GB (295 Duplicates Excluded)

Import Settings

Location: C:\Users\Nick\Pictures\[Shot Date]   Browse...

Create Subfolder(s): Shot Date (yyyy mm dd) ⌄

Rename Files: Do not rename files ⌄   +
Example: DSC_0586.JPG
☐ Preserve Current Filename in XMP

Delete Options: After Copying, Do Not Delete Originals ⌄
☐ Automatic Download 💡

Advanced Dialog   Get Media   Cancel

7 Click the **Get Media** button to download them

Hot tip

Images can also be downloaded from a USB flashdrive. To do this, connect the flashdrive and use the **From Camera or Card Reader...** download option. You will then be able to download the images in the same way as with a camera or memory card reader.

Hot tip

The Delete Options box in the Photo Downloader has options for what happens once you have downloaded your photos. These are: **After Copying, Do Not Delete Originals**; **After Copying, Verify and Delete Originals**; and **After Copying, Delete Originals**. If you do delete the originals from your camera or card reader, make sure you back up the ones that you have just downloaded, to a USB flashdrive or an external hard drive.

...cont'd

8 Click on the **Advanced Dialog** button to access additional options for downloading your images. Here, you can select specific images so that they are not all downloaded at once

Advanced Dialog

Hot tip

The Advanced Dialog Photo Downloader has an option to **Automatically Fix Red Eyes**. Check this box **On** if you want red-eye to be removed from photos as they are downloaded.

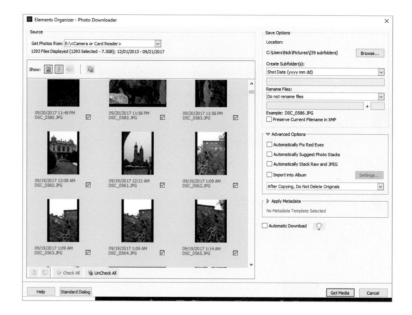

Don't forget

Depending on the number of photos that you have on your camera or memory card, the downloading process may take a few minutes.

9 Click on the **Get Media** button to import the images. They can then be viewed in the Organizer and opened in the Editor

Get Media

Hot tip

Click on the **Minimize** button in Step 9 so that you can get on with other tasks while your photos are being downloaded.

Copying - 3% Completed

From: **E:\<Camera or Card Reader>**
To: C:\Users\Nick\Pictures\2017 09 18

3%

File 40 of 1293: Copying File...

DSC_0513.JPG

Minimize   Stop

32

Importing in bulk

Using the Import function, it is also possible to import large numbers of images in one action, with the In Bulk... option:

1 From the Organizer select **Import** > **In Bulk...**

By default, the main top-level folder (Pictures) is selected, and so are all of the sub-folders.

2 In the **Import Media** window, you can select folders to import by checking the box next to them

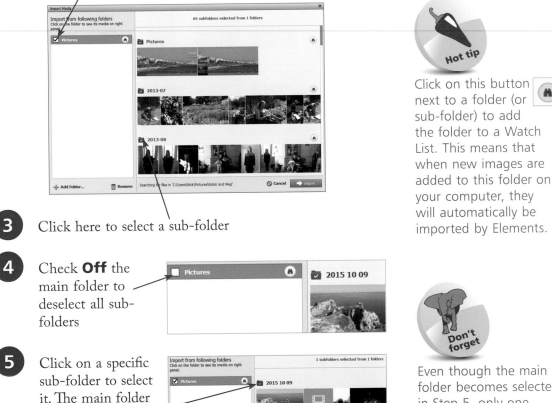

Click on this button next to a folder (or sub-folder) to add the folder to a Watch List. This means that when new images are added to this folder on your computer, they will automatically be imported by Elements.

3 Click here to select a sub-folder

4 Check **Off** the main folder to deselect all sub-folders

5 Click on a specific sub-folder to select it. The main folder is also selected

Even though the main folder becomes selected in Step 5, only one sub-folder is selected. This is shown at the top right-hand side of the window.

6 Click on the **Import** button to import the selected folders

33

Media View

Media View is the function within the Organizer that is used to view, find and sort images. When using Media View, images have to be actively added to it so it can then catalog them. Once images have been imported, Media View acts as a window for viewing and sorting your images, no matter where they are located. Media View is the default view when you access the Organizer and can be accessed at any time by clicking on the Media button:

34

Folders and Albums   Tag and Info panels

Organizer Taskbar   Keyword/Info button

There is also a magnification slider on the Taskbar, which can be used for changing the size at which images are viewed in the main Media View window:

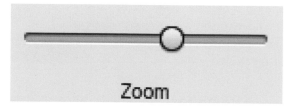

Accessing images

To access images within Media View:

 1 Click on images to select them individually, or as a group (see second Hot tip)

 2 Drag the scroll bar to scroll through images within the main window

3 Double-click on an image to view it in the whole Media View window

Hot tip

Select an image in the Organizer and select **View** > **Full Screen** from the Menu bar to view the image at the full size of your monitor.

Hot tip

To select multiple images, drag over the thumbnails, or hold down **Shift** and click on a range of thumbnails to select them all. Alternatively, hold down **Ctrl** (**Command** on a Mac) and click on the thumbnails to select a group of non-consecutive images.

35

Hot tip

If images were captured with a digital camera, they will appear in Media View in order of the date the image was taken. To make sure this is accurate, set your camera to the correct date and time.

...cont'd

Media View functionality

Media View has a considerable amount of power and functionality in terms of organizing and editing images within the Organizer. This includes the Taskbar and panels for adding tags to images, and viewing information about them:

Media View can be set to watch specific folders on your computer. Whenever images are added to these folders, or edited within them, you will be prompted to add them into the Media View. To specify the folders to be watched, select **File** > **Watch Folders** from the Menu bar and then browse to the folder, or folders, that you want to include.

The Slideshow option in the Organizer has been enhanced in Elements 2018.

When an Instant Fix is applied to a photo, a new photo is automatically created, and this is stored within a **Version Set** with the original photo. See page 39 for more details on Version Sets.

1 The Taskbar is located at the bottom of the main window and contains buttons for, from left to right: show or hide the Albums and Folders panel; undo the previous action; rotate a selected image; add images to a map for Places View; add an event to images for Event View; apply quick editing fixes; access the selected images in the Editor; and view the selected images in a slideshow

2 Select an image in the main Media View window and click on this button to apply instant editing fixes to it (without having to move to the Editor)

3 Click on one of the editing functions in the right-hand panel to apply it to the selected image(s)

...cont'd

4 Click on this button to view details of selected images in Media View

Keyword/Info

5 Click on the **Information** tab. Click on these arrows to expand each section

Tags   ● Information
▶ General
▶ Metadata
▶ History

Don't forget

For more details about adding tags to images, see pages 46-47.

6 Access the **General** panel to see information about the image name, size, date taken and where it is saved on your computer. You can edit the name and add a caption here

Tags   ● Information
▼ General
Caption:
Name: DSC_0516.JPG
Notes:

Ratings: ★ ★ ★ ★ ★
Size: 5.2MB 3072x4608
Date: 5/18/2018 12:19 AM
Location: C:\Users\Nick\Pictures\2017 09 18\
Audio: <none>

Hot tip

A caption can also be added to an image by selecting it and selecting **Edit** > **Add Caption** from the Menu bar.

37

7 Access the **Metadata** panel to see detailed information about an image that is added by the camera when it is taken

▼ Metadata
▼ FILE PROPERTIES
Filename: DSC_0516.JPG
Document Type: image/jpeg
Date Created: 1/17/20...2:32 PM
Date Modified: 1/17/20...2:38 PM
▼ CAMERA DATA (EXIF)
Make: NIKON ...RATION
Model: NIKON D3100
ISO Spe...atings: 200
Exposure Time: 1/400 sec
F-Stop: f/10
Focal Le...mm Film: 60
Focal Length: 40.00 mm
Flash: Did not fire

Don't forget

8 Click on this button to view an expanded list of Metadata information

Metadata is information about an image that is stored in the image file itself, in addition to the image that is displayed.

9 Access the **History** panel to view the editing history of the image

▼ History
Modified Date: 1/17/2018 12:38 PM
Imported On: 1/17/2018
Imported From: E:\<Camera or Card Reader>
Volume Name: Acer

Stacks

Since digital cameras make it quick, easy and cheap to capture dozens or hundreds of images on a single memory card, it is no surprise that most people are now capturing more images than ever before. One reason for this is that it is increasingly tempting to take several shots of the same subject, just to try to capture the perfect image. The one drawback with this is that when it comes to organizing your images on a computer, it can become time-consuming to work your way through all of your near-identical shots. Media View offers a useful solution to this by allowing you to stack similar images, so that you can view a single thumbnail rather than several. To do this:

You can remove images from a stack by selecting the stack in Media View and selecting **Edit** > **Stack** > **Flatten Stack** from the Menu bar. However, this will remove all of the images, apart from the top one, from Media View. This does not remove them from your hard drive, although there is an option to do this too, if you wish.

Don't forget

To revert stacked images to their original state, select the stack and select **Edit** > **Stack** > **Unstack Photos** from the Menu bar.

Beware

Only stack similar photos, otherwise you may forget which photos are underneath the stack.

 Select the images that you want to stack in Media View

 Select **Edit** > **Stack** > **Stack Selected Photos** from the Menu bar

 The images are stacked into a single thumbnail, and the existence of the stack is indicated by this icon

 To view all of the stacked images, click this button

Click here to return to the rest of the photos in Media View

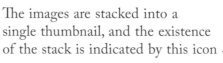

38

Version Sets

When working with digital images it is commonplace to create several different versions of a single image. This could be to use one for printing and one for use on the web, or because there are elements of an image that you want to edit. Instead of losing track of images that have been edited, it is possible to create stacked thumbnails of edited images, which are known as Version Sets. These can include the original image and all of the edited versions. Version Sets can be created and added to from the Photo Editor and viewed in Media View. To do this:

 1 Open an image in the Photo Editor

2 Make editing changes to the image in either Expert edit mode or Quick edit mode

3 Select **File** > **Save As** from the Menu bar

4 Check on the **Save in Version Set with Original** box and click **Save**

☑ Save in Version Set with Original

5 In Media View, the original image and the edited one are grouped together in a stack, and the fact that it is a Version Set is denoted by the icon in the top right-hand corner

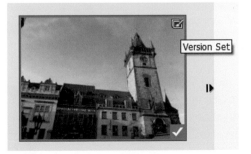
Version Set

6 To view all of the images in a Version Set, select the set and select **Edit** > **Version Set** > **Expand Items in Version Set** from the Menu bar

Don't forget

The other Version Set menu options include **Flatten Version Set**, and **Revert to Original**. The latter deletes all of the other versions except the original image.

Don't forget

Version Sets are also created if an image has an Instant Fix applied to it in the Organizer.

People View

Shots of people are popular in most types of photography. However, this can result in hundreds or thousands of photos of different people. In Elements there is a feature that enables you to tag people throughout your collections. This is known as People Recognition. To use this:

Beware

Although People Recognition is very accurate, it may, at times, identify objects that are not faces at all.

Hot tip

Select images by clicking and dragging over them, or holding down the **Ctrl** button (**Command** key on a Mac) and clicking on specific images.

Don't forget

When you access a photo at full size in Media View, you will be prompted to add a person's name if there are people in the photo.

1 In the Organizer, click on the **People** button, then click on the **Named** button

2 Any named people are shown in the **Named** window

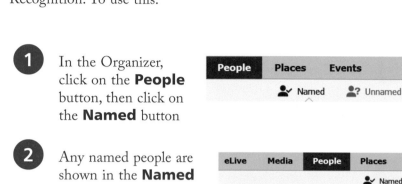

3 Click on the **Unnamed** button to view faces that have not already been assigned names

4 Click on one of the thumbnails to add a name

5 Add a name and click on the check mark symbol to apply the name to that group of photos. You can also link a photo to your Facebook friend list

Adding people directly

To add names manually, directly from a photo:

 1 Open a photo at full size in Media View and click on the **Mark Face** button

Mark Face

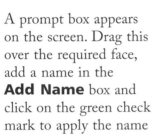 **2** A prompt box appears on the screen. Drag this over the required face, add a name in the **Add Name** box and click on the green check mark to apply the name

Add Name

Viewing people

To view people who have been tagged with People Recognition:

 1 Click on the **People** button in the main Organizer window

People

2 Click on the **Named** button. The tagged people's photos are stacked in thumbnails. Click on a thumbnail to view all of the photos of that person (that have been tagged)

People Recognition really comes into its own when you have tagged dozens or hundreds of photos. You can then view all of the photos containing a specific person.

41

Double-click on the thumbnails in the Named window to view the images in a grid. In the grid, double-click on a single image to view it at full size.

Places View

One of the most common reasons for taking photos is when people are on vacation in different and new locations. Within the Organizer it is possible to tag photos to specific locations on a map, so that you can quickly view all of your photos from a certain area. To do this:

1 In Media View, select all of the photos from a specific location

Hot tip

You can move around the map by clicking and dragging. You can also zoom in and out by right-clicking on the map and selecting the relevant command.

2 On the Taskbar, click on the **Add Location** button

3 Enter a location for the set of photos and click on the **Apply** button

4 To view photos that have been placed on a map, click on the **Places** button in the main Organizer window

Hot tip

Click on the **Unpinned** button at the top of the Places window to view all of the photos that have not had locations added to them. They appear next to the map so that they can be dragged onto a location.

...cont'd

5 Use these controls to move around the map and zoom in and out on it

Hot tip

The map can be viewed as **Map**, **Hybrid**, **Light** or **Dark**. If **Map** is selected, there is also an option for viewing **Terrain**.

6 Click on a set of photos in a location. Click on this button to move through them

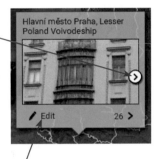

7 Click on the **Edit** button to view the individual photos in the left-hand panel

Beware

If a photo with an existing location is selected and the **Add Location** button is clicked, the location for the photo can be changed, but it will be removed from the original one.

8 Click on the **Done** button to exit the map

43

Events View

Photos in the Organizer can also be allocated to specific events such as family celebrations or overseas trips. This is done with the Events View. To do this:

 In Media View, select all of the required photos for a specific event

5/18/2018 12:19 AM   5/18/2018 12:19 AM

 On the Taskbar, click on the **Add Event** button

 In the **Add New Event** panel, add details including name, start and end date, and a description of the event

 Click on the **Done** button

To view photos that have been allocated to an event, click on the **Events** button in the main Organizer window

All photos for a specific event are grouped together

When creating a new event, photos can be added to it by dragging them into the Media Bin below the window in Step 3.

When an event is created, the event name is automatically added to the tags, which can be accessed from the Media section in the Organizer.

Click on the "i" icon on the thumbnail in the Events window to see the description for that particular event.

7 Double-click on the thumbnail to view all of the photos allocated to the event

eLive	Media	People	Places	**Events**

▦✓ Named   ▦? Suggested

< Back   ‹ Exhibition ›

★ ★ ★ ★ ★
5/18/2018 12:19 AM   ★ ★ ★ ★ ★
                           5/18/2018 12:19 AM

Hot tip

Click on the **Suggested** button at the top of the Events window to view groups of photos that Elements thinks may be suitable for new events.

8 Click on the **Back** button to go back to the thumbnail view in Step 6

< Back

9 Click on the **Calendar** to view events from specific dates

Calendar

Calendar		Clear
	All Years ▼	
Jan	Feb	Mar
Apr	May	Jun
Jul	Aug	Sep
Oct	Nov	Dec

Hot tip

Right-click on an event thumbnail to access a menu with options to edit the event; remove it; set it as a cover photo for the event thumbnail; or view it as a slideshow.

10 Click on the **Add Event** button to create another event in Event View. This is done by dragging photos into the Media Bin and entering the event details as in Step 3

Add Event

Tagging Images

As your digital image collection begins to grow on your computer, it is increasingly important to be able to keep track of your images and find the ones you want, when you want them. One way of doing this is by assigning specific tags to images. You can then search for images according to the tags that have been added to them. The tagging function is accessed from the Tags panel within Media View in the Organizer. To add tags to images:

Hot tip

When you create a new category you can also choose a new icon.

1 In Media View, click on this button on the Taskbar to show and hide the Tags panel

2 Click here to access the currently-available tags

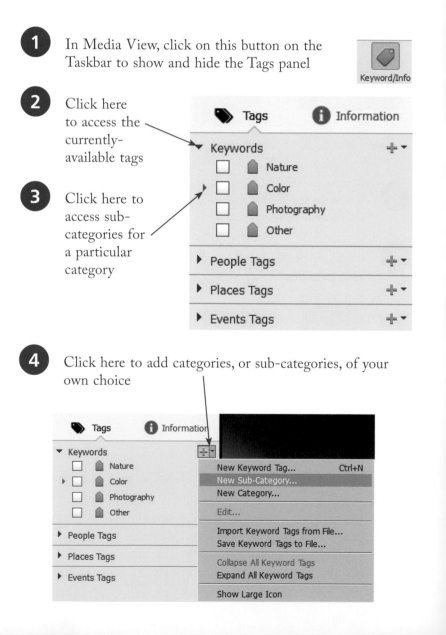

3 Click here to access sub-categories for a particular category

Don't forget

Tags can be created for People, Places and Events. They are also created when items are added to the various sections.

4 Click here to add categories, or sub-categories, of your own choice

Don't forget

Tags are also referred to as Keywords or Keyword tags.

46

5 Enter a name for the new category, or sub-category, and click on the **OK** button

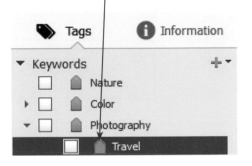

6 Select the required images from Media View

7 Drag a tag onto one of the selected images

8 The tag will be applied to all of the selected images. Each individual image will have the tag added to it

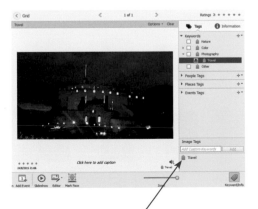

9 The images are tagged with the icon that denotes the main category, rather than the sub-category

Hot tip

Multiple tags can be added to the same image. This gives you greater flexibility when searching for images.

Don't forget

Categories can have several levels of sub-categories. To create additional levels, right-click on a sub-category and select **Create new Sub-Category** from the menu. Give the sub-category a name and ensure that the required item is selected in the **Parent Category or Sub-Category** box.

Don't forget

Tagged images can still be searched for using a sub-category tag, even though they are denoted in Media View by the tag for the main category.

Searching for Images

Once images have been tagged, they can then be searched for using those specific tags. To do this:

Using the Search box

Images can be searched for simply by typing keywords into the Search box at the top of the Organizer, in any view:

1 Click on the Search button

2 The Search window contains a Search box at the top of the window and also filter buttons down the left-hand side for conducting specific searches

3 Start typing in the Search box and click on one of the results to view all of the tagged images

4 Click on the **Grid** button to view the images in the main Organizer window

Don't forget

After returning to Grid view in Step 4, click on the **Back** button to return to the main Organizer window. Click on the **Sort By** box to sort the Search results according to Newest, Oldest, Name or Import Batch.

Using search filters

The search filter buttons on the search page can also be used to find items. To do this:

1 Click on one of the search filter buttons to view the tagged photos, which are displayed according to their tags or categories. Click on one of the thumbnails in the left-hand panel to view the photos within it, displayed in the right-hand panel

The options for search filters are: Smart Tags; People; Places; Date; Folders; Keywords; Albums; Events; Ratings; and Media Types.

2 For each selection, the filter tag is added in the Search box. Add additional tags to create multiple searches to see all items that have two or more matching tags

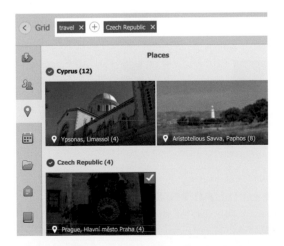

...cont'd

Searching with tags

Images can also be searched for by using the tags within the Tags panel. To do this:

Don't forget

Tags can be viewed for **Keywords**, **People Tags**, **Places Tags** and **Events Tags**.

Hot tip

If you search using a main category, any items that are within that category as a sub-category will be searched for too. If you select a sub-category, this is only what will be searched for.

Don't forget

Roll over a tag next to a photo in Media View to see a description of the Keyword tag.

1 Access the Tags panel from this button

2 Check on a box to view the images that are tagged with that keyword

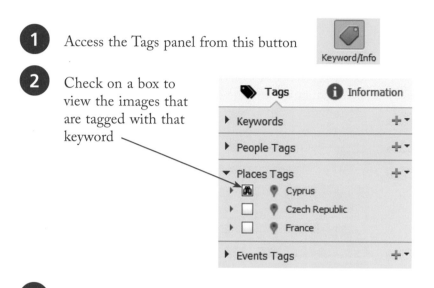

3 All matching items for a tag are shown together within the Media View window

4 Click on the **All Media** button to return to the rest of the images

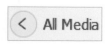

Multiple searches

Within the Tags panel it is also possible to define searches for images that have multiple (i.e. two or more) tags attached to them. To do this:

 Add a tag to an image or images, and click on the tag in the Tags panel to display all of these images (other tags that have been added to them will also be displayed next to the image)

Hot tip

Images that have been tagged within People View, Places View and Events View can also be searched for using the Keywords panel.

Don't forget

If no results are returned for a multiple search, it means that there are no images that contain all of the selected tags.

51

Add another tag to the image or images, so that there are at least two attached. Click on both of these in the Tags panel. Only the images containing both tags will be displayed

Don't forget

Two other search options are for **Visual Similarity** and **Duplicate Photos**. These display similar photos that can then be selected and placed in stacks for easier storage. It also enables you to look at similar photos and delete any that you don't want to keep. These options can be accessed by selecting **Find** > **By Visual Searches** from the Organizer Menu bar.

Albums

Albums in Elements are similar to physical photo albums: they are a location into which you can store all of your favorite groups of images. Once they have been stored there, they can easily be found when required. To create albums:

Version Sets and stacks can be added to and viewed in Albums.

1 In Media View, click here in the Albums panel and select **New Album**

2 Enter a name for the new album and choose a category if required

Click on the New Album button in Step 1 to view options for collapsing or expanding all of the albums in the panel.

3 Select the images that you would like included in the new album and drag them into the Content panel

4 Click on the **OK** button

OK

Right-click on an album name to access a menu with options to **Edit**, **Rename** or **Delete** the album.

5 The selected images are placed into the new album. Click on an album to view the images within it

Folders

One important factor in storing and searching for photos is the use of folders. Elements can replicate the folder structure that you have on your hard drive and also create new folders and edit existing ones. To work with folders in Elements:

 The available folders are listed next to the Albums section. Click on a folder to view its contents

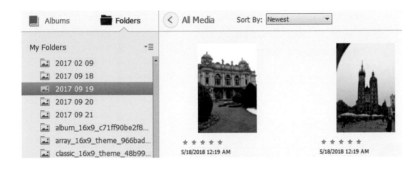

Don't forget

Even if you import a single photo, the related folder will be created within Elements, containing the photo.

2 New folders are created whenever you import photos into Elements using the **Import** > **From Files and Folders...** command

Hot tip

Right-click within the hierarchy view to add a new folder. When this is completed it also appears within your file structure on your computer's hard drive.

3 In hierarchy view, right-click on a folder to access the available options for editing it or adding a new folder

Auto Curate

Since it is easy to take hundreds or thousands of photos with a digital camera or smartphone, it can become slightly overwhelming in terms of sorting out the best ones. Within the Organizer there is a function that does this for you, by selecting the best range of photos for specific selections. This is known as Auto Curate. To use this:

Auto Curate is a new feature in Elements 2018.

Beware

Auto Curate requires a minimum of 10 photos in a group in order to perform its selection.

Don't forget

If no selection is made in Step 1, Auto Curate will search over 500 photos to find the best ones.

Don't forget

Check Off the **Auto Curate** box to return to the original view.

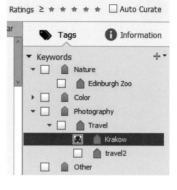

 Open the Organizer and select a group of photos, either as an Album, a Folder or by using a Keyword tag

 Check the **Auto Curate** box (above the Keywords and Info panels) to On

3 Auto Curate selects what it thinks are the best photos from the group

4 Drag the slider to show more or fewer photos for the Auto Curate selection

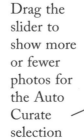

Opening and Saving Images

Once you have captured images with a digital camera or a scanner and stored them on your computer, you can open them in any of Elements' Editor modes. There are a number of options for this:

Open command

 1 Select **File** > **Open** from the Menu bar, or click on the **Open** button and select an option

 2 Select an image from your hard drive and click **Open**

Open As command

This can be used to open a file in a different file format to its original. To do this:

 1 Select **File** > **Open As** from the Menu bar

 2 Select an image and select the file format. Click **Open**

Saving images

When saving digital images, it is always a good idea to save them in at least two different file formats, particularly if layered objects such as text and shapes have been added. One of these formats should be the proprietary Photoshop format PSD or PDD. The reason for using this is that it will retain all of the layered information within an image. So, if a text layer has been added, it will still be available for editing once it has been saved and closed.

The other format that an image should be saved in is the one most appropriate for the use to which it is going to be put. Therefore, images that are going to be used on the web should be saved as JPEG, GIF or PNG files, while an image that is going to be used for printing should be saved in another format, such as TIFF. Once images have been saved in these formats, all of the layered information within them becomes flattened into a single layer and it will not be possible to edit these individual layers.

Another option for opening files is the **Open Recently Edited File** command, which is accessed from the File menu. This lists, in order, the files you have opened most recently. Some of these are also listed on the **Open** button's drop-down menu.

A proprietary file format is one that is specific to the program being used. It has greater flexibility when used within the program itself, but cannot be distributed as easily as other images.

The **Save As** command should be used if you want to make a copy of an image with a different file name.

Working with Video

As well as using Elements for viewing and organizing photos, it can also be used in the same way with video. Video can be imported into Elements in a number of ways:

- From a camera that has video-recording capabilities.

- From a digital video camera.

- From a cell/mobile phone.

- From video that has been created in the Elements Premiere program. This is a companion program to Elements and is used to manipulate and edit video. It can be bought in a package with Elements, or individually. For more details see **www.adobe.com/products/premiere-elements/**

To download video into Elements:

Elements Premiere can be bought as a package with Elements, or it can be bought individually.

Beware

Video files are usually much larger in size than photos, and if you have lots of them they will take up a lot of space on your computer.

Don't forget

To view video clips, double-click on the clip in Media View. The Elements video player will open and play the video clip.

Don't forget

To find video clips within Elements, select **Find > By Media Type > Video** from the Menu bar, and the video files will be displayed.

1 Connect the device containing the video. In the Organizer, click on the **Import** button, select the required device and download in the same way as for photos

2 The video is downloaded and displayed in the Organizer, in the same way as photos

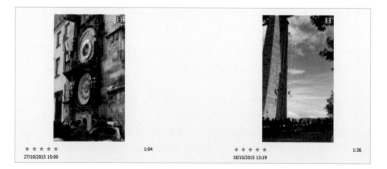

3 Video clips are identified by this symbol on their thumbnails in Media View in the Organizer

3 First Digital Steps

This chapter shows how to get up and running with digital image editing, and details some effective editing techniques for improving digital images, such as improving overall color and duplicating items.

Another Auto command on the Enhance menu is Auto Smart Fix. This can be used to automatically edit all of the color balance of an image in one step. This is also available as a panel in Quick edit mode.

The keyboard shortcut for Auto Levels is:
PC: Shift + Ctrl + L
Mac: Shift + Command
        key + L

The keyboard shortcut for Auto Contrast is:
PC: Alt + Shift + Ctrl
        + L
Mac: Alt + Shift +
        Command key + L

Two other options for color enhancement in the Toolbox are the Burn tool and the Dodge tool. The Burn tool can be dragged over areas in an image to make them darker, and the Dodge tool can be dragged over areas to make them lighter.

Color Enhancements

Some of the simplest but most effective editing changes that can be made to digital images are color enhancements. These can help to transform a mundane image into a stunning one, and Elements offers a variety of methods for achieving this. Some of these are verging towards the professional end of image editing, while others are done almost automatically by Elements. These are known as Auto adjustments, and some simple manual adjustments can also be made to the brightness and contrast of an image. All of these color enhancement features can be accessed from the Enhance menu on the Menu bar, in both Expert and Quick edit modes.

Auto Levels
This automatically adjusts the overall color tone of an image in relation to the lightest and darkest points in the image:

Auto Contrast
This automatically adjusts the contrast of an image:

...cont'd

Auto Color Correction

This automatically adjusts all of the color elements within an image:

Hot tip

The keyboard shortcut for Auto Color Correction is Shift + Ctrl + B (Shift + Command key + B on a Mac).

Adjust Brightness/Contrast

This can be used to manually adjust the brightness and contrast in an image:

1 Select **Enhance** > **Adjust Lighting** > **Brightness/Contrast** from the Menu bar (in either Expert or Quick edit mode)

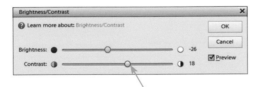

2 Drag the sliders to adjust the image's brightness and contrast

3 Click on the **OK** button

4 The brightness and contrast (and a range of other color editing functions) can also be adjusted using the panels in Quick edit mode

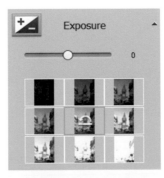

Don't forget

Alter the brightness and contrast by small amounts at a time when you are editing an image. This will help ensure that the end result does not look too unnatural.

Hot tip

Always make sure that the Preview box is checked when you are applying color enhancements. This will display the changes as you make them, and before they are applied to the image.

59

Hot tip

Adjusting shadows can make a significant improvement to an image in which one area is under-exposed and the rest is correctly exposed.

Don't forget

Shadows and highlights can also be adjusted in the Levels panel: **Enhance** > **Adjust Color** > **Levels** from the Menu bar. See pages 112-115 for more details about Levels.

Beware

Some digital cameras have a tendency to create slightly darker images, so adjusting the Shadows/Highlights is always a good option.

...cont'd

Adjust Shadows/Highlights

One problem that most photographers encounter at some point is when part of an image is exposed correctly, while another part is either over- or under-exposed. If this is corrected using general color correction techniques such as adjusting levels of brightness and contrast, the poorly-exposed area may be improved, but at the expense of the area that was correctly exposed initially. To overcome this, the Shadows/Highlights command can be used to adjust particular tonal areas of an image. To do this:

1 Open an image where parts of the image, or all of it, are incorrectly exposed

2 Select **Enhance** > **Adjust Lighting** > **Shadows/ Highlights** from the Menu bar

3 Make the required adjustments by dragging the sliders

4 Click on the **OK** button

5 The poorly-exposed areas of the image have been corrected

Cropping

Cropping is a technique that can be used to remove unwanted areas of an image and highlight the main subject. The area to be cropped can only be selected as a rectangle. To crop an image:

1 Select the **Crop** tool from the Toolbox

2 Click and drag on an image to select the area to be cropped. The area that is selected is retained and the area to be cropped appears grayed-out

3 Click and drag on these markers to resize the crop area

4 Click on the check mark to accept the changes, or the circle to reject them

The different crop options are all accessed from the Tool Options bar.

The Tool Options for the Crop tool have an option for selecting pre-set sizes for the Crop tool. This results in the crop being in specific proportions; e.g. 10 x 8 inches. Click on the down-pointing arrow in the No Restriction box and select an option.

When cropping photos it is also possible to use various overlay grids to help the composition of the image. One of these is the Rule of Thirds, whereby the cropped area is based on a 3x3 grid, with the main subjects positioned at the intersecting points of the gridlines.

...cont'd

Perspective cropping

Due to the way some lenses are constructed on digital cameras, tall buildings can sometimes look distorted (and also at slight angles). This can be amended using the Perspective Crop tool:

 Open the image to be amended

 Select the **Perspective Crop** tool from the Crop Tool Options

Drag the Perspective Crop tool around the required area, in the same way as for a regular crop

Drag the top corners of the crop area to specify the dimensions for the selected area (dragging the corners outwards narrows the perspective). Click on the green check mark symbol to apply the perspective crop

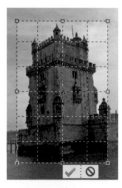

To simplify the crop function, there are a range of auto crop options, where the suggested crop area is displayed using a range of preset options. To use these, select the **Crop** tool. The auto crop options are displayed on four buttons in the Tool Options panel. Click on an option to select it and click on the green check mark to accept the suggested crop area, or click on the red circle to reject the suggestion.

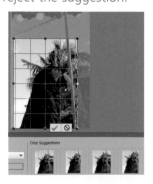

Healing Brush

One of the most popular techniques in digital imaging is removing unwanted items, particularly physical blemishes such as spots and wrinkles. This can be done with the Clone tool but the effects can sometimes be too harsh, as a single area is copied over the affected item. A more subtle effect can be achieved with the Healing Brush and the Spot Healing Brush tools. The Healing Brush can be used to remove blemishes over larger areas such as wrinkles:

1 Open an image with blemishes covering a reasonably large area; i.e. more than a single spot

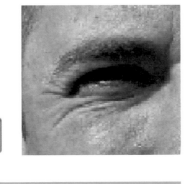

2 Select the **Healing Brush** tool from the Toolbox and make the required selections in the Tool Options bar

3 Hold down **Alt** and click on an area of the image to load the Healing Brush tool. Drag over the affected area. The cross is the area that is copied beneath the circle. At this point the overall tone is not perfect and looks too pink

4 Release the mouse, and the Healing Brush blends the affected area with the one that was copied over it. This creates a much more natural skin tone

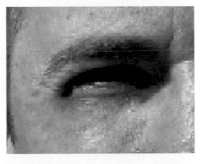

Hot tip

The Healing Brush tool can be more subtle than the Clone tool, as it blends the copied area together with the area over which it is copying. This is particularly effective on images of people, as it preserves the overall skin tone better than the Clone tool does.

Hot tip

The Spot Healing Brush tool can be used to remove items such as small blemishes or spots. Click on this button in the Healing Brush Tool Options bar and drag it over the affected area to remove it.

Hot tip

When dragging over a blemish with the Spot Healing Brush tool, make sure the brush size is larger than the area of the blemish. This will ensure that you can cover the blemish in a single stroke.

63

Cloning

Cloning is a technique that can be used to copy one area of an image over another. This can be used to cover up small imperfections in an image, such as a dust mark or a spot, and also to copy or remove large items in an image, such as a person.

To clone items:

1 Select the **Clone Stamp** tool from the Toolbox

2 Set the Clone Stamp options in the Tool Options bar

3 Hold down Alt, and then click and hold on the image to select a source point from which the cloning will start

4 Drag the cursor to copy everything over which the selection point marker passes

Pattern Cloning

The Pattern Stamp tool can be used to copy a selected pattern over an image, or onto a selected area of an image. To do this:

 Select the **Pattern Stamp** tool from the Toolbox

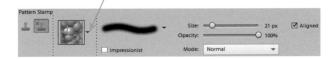

Click here in the Tool Options bar to access the available patterns

The Pattern Stamp tool is grouped in the Toolbox with the Clone Stamp tool. It can be selected from the Tool Options panel if the Clone Stamp tool is selected.

Select a pattern for the Pattern Stamp tool

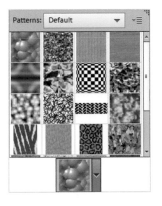

Click and drag on an image to copy the selected pattern over it

Patterns can be added to the Patterns panel by selecting an image, or an area of an image, and selecting **Edit > Define Pattern** from the Editor Menu bar. Then, give the pattern a name in the **Pattern Name** dialog box, and click **OK**.

Rotating

Various rotation commands can be applied to images, and also individual layers in layered images. This can be useful for positioning items and also for correcting the orientation of an image that is on its side or upside down.

Rotating a whole image

 Select **Image** > **Rotate** from the Menu bar

 Select a rotation option from the menu

 Select **Custom...** to enter your own value for the amount you want an image rotated

90° Left
90° Right
180°
Custom...
Flip Horizontal
Flip Vertical
Free Rotate Layer
Rotate Layer 90° Left
Rotate Layer 90° Right
Rotate Layer 180°
Flip Layer Horizontal
Flip Layer Vertical
Straighten and Crop Image
Straighten Image

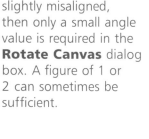

Rotate Canvas

Angle: 5   ● °Right   ○ °Left   OK   Cancel

 Click the **OK** button

Rotating a layer
To rotate separate layers within an image:

 Open an image that consists of two or more layers. Select one of the layers in the Layers panel

 Select **Image** > **Rotate** from the Menu bar

Select a layer rotation option from the menu

The selected layer is rotated independently

Transforming

The Transform commands can be used to resize an image, and to apply some basic distortion techniques. These commands can be accessed by selecting **Image** > **Transform** from the Menu bar.

Free Transform

This enables you to manually alter the size and shape of an image. To do this:

1 Select **Image** > **Transform** > **Free Transform** from the Menu bar

2 Click and drag here to transform the vertical and horizontal size of the image. Hold down **Shift** to transform it in proportion

Click just outside this placeholder and drag left or right to manually rotate an image with the Transform function.

The other options from the Transform menu are Skew, Distort and Perspective. These can be accessed and applied in a similar way to the Free Transform option.

Magnification

In Elements there are a number of ways in which the magnification at which an image is being viewed can be increased or decreased. This can be useful if you want to zoom in on a particular part of an image for editing purposes, or if you want to view a whole image to see the result of editing effects that have been applied.

View menu

Don't forget

The View menu can be used to display rulers at the top and left of an image, which can be useful for precise measurements and placement. There is also a command for displaying a grid over the top of the whole image.

Hot tip

The keyboard shortcut for zooming in is:
PC: Ctrl + =
Mac: Command key + =

The keyboard shortcut for zooming out is:
PC: Ctrl + -
Mac: Command key + -

 Select **View** from the Menu bar and select one of the options from the View menu

View	Window	Help
New Window for bulgaria4.jpg		
Zoom In		Ctrl+=
Zoom Out		Ctrl+-
Fit on Screen		Ctrl+0
Actual Pixels		Ctrl+1
Print Size		
Selection		Ctrl+H
Rulers		Shift+Ctrl+R
Grid		Ctrl+'

Zoom tool

 Select the **Zoom** tool from the Toolbox

2 Click once on an image to enlarge it (usually by 100% each time). Hold down **Alt** and click to decrease the magnification

Hot tip

Click and drag with the Zoom tool over a small area to increase the magnification to the maximum; i.e. 3200%. This can be particularly useful when performing close-up editing tasks, such as removing red-eye.

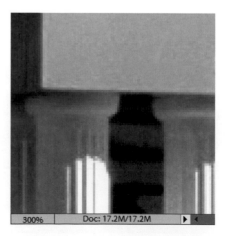

300% | Doc: 17.2M/17.2M

...cont'd

Navigator panel

This can be used to move around an image and also magnify certain areas. To use the Navigator panel:

1 Access the **Navigator** panel by selecting **Window** > **Navigator** from the Menu bar

2 Drag this slider to magnify the area of the image within the red rectangle

Zoom: — ⬤——— **+** 34.45%

3 Drag the rectangle to change the area of the image that is being magnified

Hot tip

The keyboard shortcut for accessing the Navigator panel is F12.

Don't forget

The Navigator panel also has buttons for zooming in and out. These are located at the left and right of the slider.

Hot tip

Click on different areas on the thumbnail in the Navigator panel to view these areas in the main Editor window.

Eraser

The Eraser tool can be used to remove areas of an image. In a simple, single layer image this can just leave a blank hole, which has to be filled with something. The Eraser options are:

- **Eraser**, which can be used to erase part of the background image or a layer within it.

- **Background Eraser**, which can be used to remove an uneven background.

- **Magic Eraser**, which can be used to quickly remove a solid background (see below).

Erasing a background

With the Magic Eraser tool it is possible to delete a colored background in an image. To do this:

The Background Eraser tool can be used to remove an uneven background. To do this, drag over the background with the Background Eraser tool and, depending on the settings in the Tool Options panel, everything that it is dragged over will be removed.

1 Open an image with an evenly-colored background

2 Select the **Magic Eraser** and make the required selections in the Tool Options bar. Make sure the Contiguous box is not checked

3 Click once on the background. It is removed from the image, regardless of where it occurs

If the **Contiguous** box is not checked, the background color will be removed wherever it occurs in the image. If the Contiguous box is checked, the background color will only be removed where it touches another area of the same color that is not broken by another element of the image.

4 Quick Wins

This chapter looks at some of the "quick wins" that can be done in Elements, such as removing unwanted objects, changing photos to black and white, and improving hazy photos. It also shows some of the Guided and Quick edit options that provide step-by-step actions for creating a range of creative and striking photos. This includes adding items to photos, such as frames, textures, filters and graphics.

Removing Red-Eye

The best way to deal with red-eye is to avoid it in the first place. Try using a camera that has a red-eye reduction function.

There is also an option in the Red Eye Removal tool for removing red-eye from pets.

Red-eye can also be removed when images are being downloaded from the camera. This is an option in the Photo Downloader window.

Red-eye can be removed automatically by clicking on the **Auto Correct** button in the Red Eye Removal Tool Options panel.

Red Eye Removal

Auto Correct

One of the most common problems with photographs of people, whether they are taken digitally or with a film-based camera, is red-eye. This is caused when the camera's flash is used, which then reflects in the subject's pupils. This can create the dreaded red-eye effect, where the subject can unintentionally be transformed into a demonic character.

Elements has recognized that removing red-eye is one of the top priorities for most amateur photographers, and a specific tool for this purpose has been included in the Toolbox: the Red Eye Removal tool. This is available in Expert or Quick edit modes:

1 Open an image that contains red-eye

2 Select the **Zoom** tool from the Toolbox

3 Drag around the affected area until it appears at a suitable magnification. Select the **Red Eye Removal** tool from the Toolbox

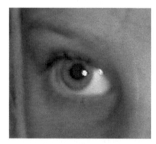

4 Click in the Tool Options bar to select the size of the pupil and the amount by which it will be darkened

5 Click once on the red-eye, or drag around the affected area to remove the red-eye

Changing to Black and White

Most digital cameras and scanners are capable of converting color images into black and white at the point of capture. However, it is also possible to use Elements to convert existing color images into black-and-white ones. To do this:

1 Open a color image and select **Enhance > Convert to Black and White** from the Menu bar

2 The Convert to Black and White dialog box has various options for how the image is converted

3 Select the type of black-and-white effect to be applied, depending on the subject in the image

4 Drag these sliders to specify the intensity of the effect to be applied for different elements

5 Click on the **OK** button

6 The image is converted into black and white, according to the settings that have been selected

Hot tip

The keyboard shortcut to access the Convert to Black and White dialog window is Alt + Ctrl + B (Alt + Command key + B on a Mac).

Hot tip

A similar effect can be achieved by selecting **Enhance > Adjust Color > Remove Color** from the Menu bar.

Don't forget

The Guided edits also have an option for turning photos into black and white: **Guided > Black & White > Black and White**.

Quickly Removing Items

One of the most annoying aspects of taking photos is to capture what you think is a perfect image, only to find that there is an unwanted object in the final shot. In Elements, it is possible to delete unwanted items and automatically fill in the area from where these are removed. To do this:

Several different items can be removed from the same photo. To do this, select each one separately and perform the actions from Step 3 onwards.

The selection around the object does not have to be too accurate, as long as it goes around the border of the object.

If an area is selected and then deleted it will leave a blank space, filled with either the color palette's background or foreground color.

 Open an image that contains an unwanted object

 Use one of the selection tools to select the unwanted object

Lasso

 Select **Edit** > **Fill Selection...** from the Menu bar

Edit	Image	Enhance	Layer
Undo Lasso			Ctrl+Z
Redo Fill			Ctrl+Y
Revert			Shift+Ctrl+A
Cut			Ctrl+X
Copy			Ctrl+C
Copy Merged			Shift+Ctrl+C
Paste			Ctrl+V
Paste Into Selection			Shift+Ctrl+V
Delete			
Fill Selection...			

74

4 Make the selections in the Fill Layer dialog box. Ensure **Content-Aware** is selected

Fill Layer

Learn more about: Fill Layer

Use: Content-Aware

Blending
Mode: Normal
Opacity: 100 %
Preserve Transparency

OK
Cancel

5 Click on the **OK** button

6 The selection is deleted and the area is automatically filled with the background

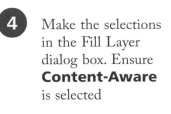

If there are too many colors around the selected area, the fill effect may appear inaccurate. If this is the case, try with a slightly different selection area.

7 The final image makes it appear as if the unwanted object was never there in the first place

Zoom in to the final image to make sure that the background has been filled as accurately as possible.

Moving Items in a Photo

Unless you are taking photos under studio conditions, it is probable that you will get some unwanted items in your photos, or the composition may not be exactly as you would like it in terms of the position of the subjects. The answer to this is the Content-Aware editing tool. This can be used to move subjects in a photo and then have the background behind them filled in automatically.

Hot tip

In the Content-Aware Move Options panel, drag the **Healing** slider to specify how the edited area blends with the rest of the image.

 Open an image with a subject that you want to move

Don't forget

When moving items, it is most effective when the background has a reasonable amount of solid or similar colors.

2 Select the **Content-Aware Move** tool from the Toolbox

 Select the **Move** radio button in Tool Options

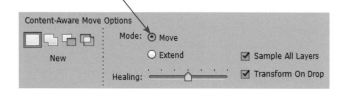

4 Drag around the subject that you want to move

Hot tip

The Content-Aware Move selection area can be moved by using the arrow keys on the keyboard; e.g. left and right, up and down.

76

5 Drag the subject to a new position

The subject can be positioned anywhere in the photo.

6 The area where the subject was previously located is filled in by the Content-Aware function

The Content-Aware tool can also be used to extend areas within an image. To do this, check on the **Extend** box in Tool Options, drag around the area you want to extend, and then drag the selection into place. The Content-Aware Move tool will automatically fill in the background for the area that is extended.

Improving Expressions

Taking photos of people is a very common use for digital cameras. However, sometimes the end result is not quite as expected: perhaps the subject is not smiling enough, or has their eyes half-closed. In Elements 2018 it is possible to adjust these imperfections so that all of your portraits look their best. To do this:

Don't forget

The circle around the face in Step 1 is preset and cannot be moved or resized. It serves to show the face that is selected.

Beware

Make small facial adjustments at a time, otherwise the final image may end up looking like a caricature.

Hot tip

If there is more than one person in a photo, click on each one to select them and adjust their features. Only one person can be selected at a time, and when they are selected, the circle in Step 1 appears around their face.

Don't forget

Click on the **Reset** button to return to the original, unaltered image.

Reset

1 Open the image containing the expression that you want to edit. In either Quick or Expert edit mode, select **Enhance** > **Adjust Facial Features** from the Menu bar

2 Drag the sliders to amend the elements of the facial expression. This can be done for **Lips**, **Eyes**, **Nose** and **Face** options

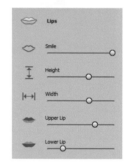

3 As the changes are made, they are reflected in the subject's face (if the **After** button is selected)

4 Click on the **OK** button to apply the facial adjustment changes

OK

Removing Haze

Despite our best efforts, some photos do not come out the way we hoped. One problem can be that photos appear hazy, which is often accompanied by a washed-out sky. To remedy this:

1 Open a photo that is suffering from a hazy effect

2 Select **Enhance > Haze Removal** from the Menu bar in Expert or Quick edit mode

3 The Haze Removal window displays the image

4 Drag this slider to apply the haze removal effect

5 Drag this slider to apply the degree of the effect

Haze removal is a good option for landscape photos that have been taken in dull lighting.

Toggle the **Before/ After** button at the bottom of the Haze Removal window to view the two states of the image.

There is also an Auto Haze Removal option that can be accessed from the Menu bar in Expert or Quick edit mode: **Enhance > Auto Haze Removal**.

Opening Closed Eyes

Taking photos of people can be a frustrating business: you think you have captured the perfect shot, only to find that one or more of your subjects has their eyes closed. Thankfully, with Elements 2018 these types of photos can be edited by opening any closed eyes in the shot. To do this:

Opening closed eyes in a photo is a new feature in Elements 2018.

The number of photos being displayed in Step 4 can be filtered by selecting to show items from a specific Album, or by People, Places, Events or Keyword tags.

 Open a photo that has a subject with closed eyes

2 Select **Enhance** > **Open Closed Eyes** from the Menu bar in Expert or Quick edit mode

3 Select a location to choose an image with open eyes for the subject; e.g. the Organizer or from your computer

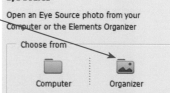

Eye Source

Open an Eye Source photo from your Computer or the Elements Organizer

Choose from

Computer   Organizer

 Select the required images and click on the **Add Selected Photos** button

Add Selected Photos

Click on the **Done** button

 The selected images are added to the Eye Source panel

All of the people included in the images selected in Step 4 are included in the Eye Source panel.

7 Click on a suitable image with open eyes for the subject

8 The selection from the Eye Source panel replaces the closed eyes of the subject

Once new eyes have been added to a subject, they can be also be edited using the Adjust Facial Features function (see page 78), or normal image-editing functions, such as the Spot Healing Brush or cloning.

9 Click on the **Reset** button to start again, or the **OK** button to apply the change

Quick Edit Mode Options

The Quick edit options in Elements offer a number of functions within the one location. This makes it easier to apply a number of techniques at the same time.

Using Quick edit mode

82

 Open an image in the Editor and click on the **Quick** button

 The Quick edit mode has a modified Toolbox with fewer tools, which is displayed here

 Click on the bottom toolbar to access the Quick edit panel options. The default one is for **Adjustments**

 Click on the **Adjustments** panel to make the appropriate changes (see pages 84-85)

Quick Edit Toolbox

The Quick edit Toolbox has a reduced Toolbox that includes:

- Zoom tool
- Hand tool
- Quick Selection tool
- Red-Eye Removal tool
- Whiten Teeth tool
- Straighten tool
- Text tool
- Spot Healing/Healing tool
- Crop tool
- Move tool

Hot tip

To show or hide the Quick edit Toolbox (and also the Expert edit Toolbox) select **Window** > **Tools** from the Menu bar.

Beware

The Red-Eye Removal tool is the same as the one in Expert mode, which includes the Pet Eye option for removing red-eye in photos of pets.

Whitening teeth

One of the tool options in the Quick edit mode Toolbox is for whitening teeth in a photo. To do this:

 Open a relevant image and click on the **Whiten Teeth** tool, and select a brush size for the tool

2 Drag the Whiten Teeth tool over the teeth

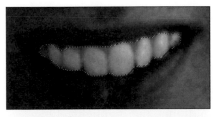

3 The teeth area is selected and whitened in one operation

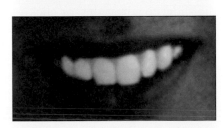

Beware

Do not overdo the teeth whitening effect, otherwise it will start to look unnatural.

Quick Edit Adjustments

The adjustment panels in the Quick edit section are:

Changes are displayed in the main Quick edit window in real time, as they are being made.

Smart Fix panel

This performs several editing changes in a single operation. Click on the Auto button to have the changes applied automatically, or drag the slider to specify the extent of the editing changes. Click on the thumbnails to apply preset amounts of the change.

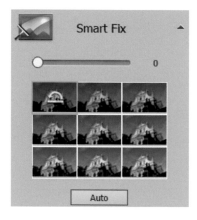

The Exposure panel is a good option for quickly editing photos that are under- or over-exposed; i.e. too dark or too light.

Exposure panel

This provides options for adjusting the lighting and contrast in an image. Drag the sliders to adjust the exposure, or click on one of the thumbnails to apply a preset option.

Shadows and highlights can be edited within Expert edit mode:
Enhance > Adjust Lighting > Shadows/ Highlights.

Lighting panel

This provides options for adjusting the lightest and darkest points in an image. This is done by adjusting the shadows, midtones and highlights. Drag the slider to adjust this, or click on one of the thumbnails for an auto option.

...cont'd

Color panel

Click on the Auto button to automatically adjust the hue and saturation of an image, or drag the slider to make manual adjustments. Click on the thumbnails to apply preset amounts.

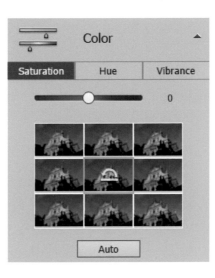

Balance panel

Drag the slider to adjust the warmth of the colors of an image and the color balance. Click on the thumbnails to apply preset amounts.

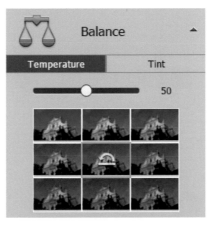

Sharpen panel

This can be used to apply sharpening to an image to make it clearer: either automatically with the Auto button; with the panel thumbnails; or manually with the slider.

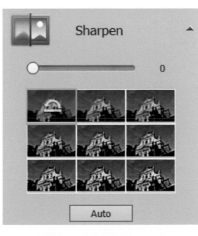

The Balance panel can be used to create some abstract color effects.

Sharpening works by increasing the contrast between adjoining pixels to make the overall image appear more in focus. It can also be accessed by selecting **Enhance** > **Auto Sharpen** or **Enhance** > **Unsharp Mask** from the Expert Menu bar. The Unsharp Mask option has a dialog window where the effect can be added as a percentage.

Enhancing with Quick Edits

In addition to the Adjustments option, the other buttons on the Quick edit toolbar are for adding Effects, Textures and Frames to your photos. They can be used individually or in combination, to enhance your photos so that they will really stand out for your family and friends. To begin, open the image that you want to enhance with the Quick edit options:

Effects

To add photo effects to your images:

The Effects panel has sub-categories for the main categories; i.e. the Seasons category has Summer, Autumn, Winter and Snow. Move the cursor over a category and click on the down-pointing arrow to view the sub-categories.

The Effects panel also has a Smart Looks option with five preset options for your photos.

1 Click on the **Effects** button on the Quick edit toolbar

Effects

2 Click on one of the Effects options to apply that effect to the currently-active image

Click on this button at the top of the Effects panel to reset the image to its original state, regardless of how many different options have been selected from the Effects panel.

...cont'd

Textures

To add texture effects to your images:

 Click on the **Textures** button on the Quick edit toolbar

 Click on one of the Textures options to apply that to the currently-active image

Frames

To add frame effects to your images:

 Click on the **Frames** button on the Quick edit toolbar

 Click on one of the Frames options to apply that to the currently-active image

The effects are added to the image:

Beware

Textures are applied as an effect on the currently-open image; they cover the image as a separate layer.

Hot tip

Save the file in a .PSD or .PDD format (a proprietary Photoshop format) to preserve the items added in Quick edit mode, so that they can be edited again when the file is opened. Save it in a .JPEG format to merge all of the layers, in which case they will not be able to be edited separately.

Hot tip

Use the options on these two pages for creative effects, particularly if you want to create items such as photo cards.

Adding Filters

Filters are an excellent option for adding a range of effects to photos. They can be accessed and applied from the Menu bar in Expert or Quick edit mode, or the toolbar in Expert edit mode:

1 In Expert edit mode, open the photo to which you want to apply a filter effect, and click on the **Filters** panel button

2 Click on a filter effect and use the sliders to determine the settings for the filter. Click on the green check mark symbol to apply the filter effect

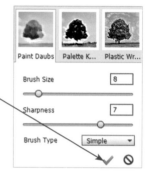

88

3 Alternatively, in Expert or Quick edit mode, click on the **Filter** button on the Menu bar, and select a filter category and sub-category

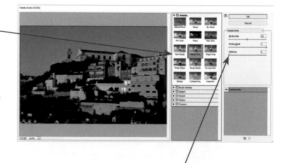

4 Each category has preset options. Click on one to apply this to the photo

5 Most filters have sliders that can be used to edit the effect that is being applied. After you have made the desired changes, click on the **OK** button

Adding Graphics

In Expert edit mode it is possible to add a wide range of graphical elements to an image. To do this:

 1 Click on the **Graphics** panel button

 2 At the top of the Graphics panel, click on the **Show All** drop-down menus to select categories and sub-categories

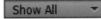

Show All

Show All ▼
Backgrounds
Frames
Graphics
Shapes
Text
Show All

Show All ▼
By Type
By Activity
By Color
By Event
By Mood
By Object
By Seasons
By Style
By Word
Show All

3 Graphical shapes can be dragged onto an image, on a new layer, and then resized within the image by clicking on them and dragging the resizing handles

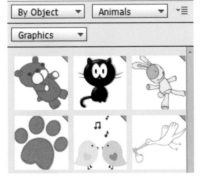

4 Backgrounds can be dragged onto an image as a new layer, and the rest of the content can interact with the background through the application of layer masks or opacity (see pages 142-145)

Beware

There are hundreds of graphics that can be used, but try not to add too many to a single image as it may become too cluttered.

Hot tip

Click on the **Layers** panel button after graphics have been added to see how this affects the construction of the image.

Using Guided Edit Mode

In Elements, the Guided edit function has been enhanced to make it easier to perform both simple editing functions, and also more complex image-editing processes that consist of a number of steps. To use the various functions of Guided edit mode:

 Open an image and click on the **Guided** button

 Click on the buttons at the top of the Guided edits window to view the different categories

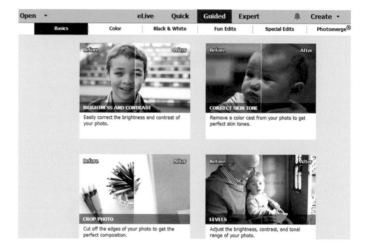

 Items in each category have a thumbnail image that shows the **Before** and **After** effects for each item. Drag the slider across the thumbnail to view the effect for a greater or lesser amount of the thumbnail

90

Applying Guided edits

The process for Guided edits is the same regardless of the type of edit that has been selected:

1 Apply the Guided edit effect that has been selected. Different categories have varying numbers of steps; the **Basics** category has the fewest number of steps

For details of some of the Guided edit options, see Chapter 5.

Enhance Colors

Click Auto to balance the colors and contrast in the photo.

Auto Fix

Use the sliders below to fine tune the adjustment.

Hue :
Saturation :
Lightness :

2 Click on the **Next** button once the Guided edits have been completed, to save the final image

Next

If you do not like an effect that has been applied, click on the **Cancel** button.

3 Specify how you want to save and/or share the final image

Enhance Colors

What would you like to do next?

Save:

Save   Save As

Continue Editing:

In Quick   In Expert

Share:

f Facebook

●● Flickr

Twitter

Click on the **Save** button to save the final image with the same file name, and in the same file format (this overwrites the original). Click on the **Save As** button to save it as a new image with either a new file name or in a new file format, or both.

4 Click on the **Done** button

Done

Photomerge Effects

Within Elements there are a number of Photomerge effects that can be used to combine elements from different photos to create a new image. This can be used to remove items from photos, combine elements from two or more photos, and match the exposure from different photos.

To access the Photomerge options, select **Guided** edit mode and click on the **Photomerge** tab.

The Photomerge options are:

- **Compose**. This can be used to merge a part of one image with the background of another. This is a good option if you want to include people from one photo and transfer them into another photo.

- **Exposure**. This can be used to create a well-exposed photo from a series of photos of the same shot that have different exposures; i.e. one may be over-exposed and another under-exposed. The Photomerge effect combines the photos so that the final one is correctly exposed. This can be done with the **Automatic** option, or the **Manual** one.

- **Faces**. This is an option for combining features of two faces together. This is done by opening photos of two people and then aligning the features of one so that they are merged with the other. This is a fun effect that can be used to combine faces of family members or two friends.

- **Group Shot**. This can be used to add or delete people from group shots. This is done by opening two or more photos of the group. Use the **Pencil** tool to merge a person from one photo into the other, and the **Eraser** tool to delete any areas that you do not want copied to the new photo.

- **Scene Cleaner**. This can be used to remove any unwanted elements in a photo. This is done by using two or more similar photos with elements that you want to remove, then merging the elements that you want to keep into the final photo. This is a good option if a single object has spoilt what is otherwise a good photo.

- **Panorama**. This can be used to create panoramas with two or more photos (see pages 93-94 for details).

For the Exposure Photomerge function, all of the photos used have to be of exactly the same shot, otherwise there will be some overlap in the final image.

The Pencil tool is used for several of the Photomerge options. It is used to draw over an area in a source image that is then merged into the final image.

Creating Panoramas

For anyone who takes landscape pictures, sooner or later the desire to create a panorama occurs. With film-based cameras, this usually involves sticking several photographs together to create the panorama, albeit a rather patchwork one. With digital images, the end result can look a lot more professional, and Elements has a dedicated function for achieving this: the Photomerge Panorama.

When creating a panorama there are a few rules to follow:

- If possible, use a tripod to ensure that your camera stays at the same level for all of the shots.

- Keep the same exposure settings for all images.

- Make sure that there is a reasonable overlap between images (about 20%). Some cameras enable you to align the correct overlap between the images.

- Keep the same distance between yourself and the object you are capturing, otherwise the end result will look out of perspective.

To create a panorama:

 In Expert edit mode, open two or more images and select **Guided** > **Photomerge** > **Photomerge Panorama** from the Menu bar

2 Click on the **Auto Panorama** button to create the panorama automatically from the selected images

3 Click on the **Create Panorama** button

Do not include too many images in a panorama, otherwise it could be too large for viewing or printing easily.

Panoramas do not just have to be of landscapes. They can also be used for items such as a row of buildings, or crowds at a sporting event.

In Step 2 there are other options for the style of the panorama.

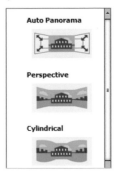

...cont'd

 The panorama will be created, but with gaps where the images could not be matched. The **Clean Edges** dialog box asks if you would like to fill in the edges of the panorama. Click on the **Yes** button to blend the empty areas with the background

 Panoramas can usually be improved by applying color correction such as Brightness/Contrast and Shadows/Highlights. They can also be cropped to make a narrower panorama to highlight the main subject

5 Artistic Effects

This chapter shows how to create stunning effects and features, to give your photos the "wow" factor. This is done with Guided edit mode where there are numerous templates to follow for dazzling effects.

Photo Text

Creating text from a photo is a great way to produce creative messages or posters. To do this:

 Open the image that you want to use as the basis of the Photo Text

 Access Guided edit mode and in the **Fun Edits** section, click on the **Photo Text** button

 Click on the **Type Tool** button

 Select the required formatting options for the Type Tool

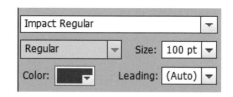

 Click on the photo and type the required text

 Click on this button to apply the effect and create the Photo Text

7 Select an option for how the text fills the photo

8 Select an option for a background for the text

9 Click on the **Crop Image** button to crop the Photo Text and remove any unwanted space

10 Click on these buttons to add a bevel effect to the text

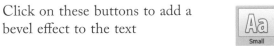

The fill options in Step 7 do not need to be applied, in which case the Photo Text will retain its original size.

11 Click on the **Advanced** button to refine the options for the text style

Advanced

The Advanced options for editing the text style include the lighting angle, drop shadow, bevel, and stroke size.

12 Click on the **Next** button

Next

13 Select an option for saving the Photo Text, or continue editing it

Photo Text

What would you like to do next?

Save:

| Save | Save As |

Continue Editing:

| In Quick | In Expert |

Below the visible options in Step 13 are also options for sharing the current project to Facebook, Flickr or Twitter. These are standard options for Guided edits.

14 Click on the **Done** button

Done

Effects Collage

Individual photos can be quickly and effectively turned into impressive collages in Elements 2018. To do this:

 1 Open the image that you want to turn into a collage

2 Access Guided edit mode and in the **Fun Edits** section, click on the **Effects Collage** button

3 Select an option for a layout of the collage; e.g. how the photo is split up

Hot tip

The option for continuing editing in Expert edit mode (as in Step 13 on the previous page) is a good way to see the composition of a Guided edit mode image. Click on the **Layers** panel button on the Expert edit mode bottom toolbar to view the layers used to create the image.

4 Select a style for the collage. Click on the down-pointing arrow to access the full range of styles

5 Click on the **Next** button to complete the collage and save, edit or share it as shown on page 97

Painterly Effect

The Painterly effect is one that creates a border around an image to make it look like it has been painted on a canvas. To do this:

 1 Open the image for the Painterly effect

 **2** Access Guided edit mode and in the **Fun Edits** section, click on the **Painterly** button

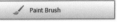 **3** Click on the **Paint Brush** button and click on the photo to apply the template each time

 4 Select a color for the background canvas. Click on the **Select Custom Color** button to select a color other than black or white

Texture and Effect are optional for adding to the background.

5 Select a texture for the background color and an effect for it

_fx_ Effect

If a texture is added, the **Opacity** slider can be used to determine how much of the textured background is visible.

6 Click on the **Next** button to complete the Painterly effect and save, edit or share it as shown on page 97

Speed Pan

The Speed Pan effect is a great way to create the effect of motion, and give a photo a dynamic appearance. To do this:

 Open the image to which you want to add the effect of speed

Hot tip

Use the Zoom tool in the Guided edit mode Toolbox to show the subject to be selected in Step 3 at a large size, so that the selection can be as accurate as possible.

 Access Guided edit mode and in the **Fun Edits** section, click on the **Speed Pan** button

 Click on the **Quick Selection Tool** button and drag it over the part of the image that you want to remain static

 Click on the **Add Motion Blur** button and apply the setting for the amount and direction of motion blur to be added to the background of the image

Hot tip

Click on the **Undo** button on the bottom toolbar to undo actions that have been applied to an image, for any of the Guided edit mode options.

 Click on the **Refine Effect Brush** button to fine tune the selection against the background

Click on the **Next** button to complete the Speed Pan effect and save, edit or share it as shown on page 97

Frame Creator

Elements 2018 comes with its own range of frames for photos, but you can create your own too. To do this:

1 Open the image that you want to use to create your own photo frame

2 Access Guided edit mode and in the **Special Edits** section, click on the **Frame Creator** button

3 Use one of the selection tools to select an area of the image (this will be used to create the space for a photo to be inserted – the surrounding area will be the frame)

Hot tip

To add a photo to your own frame, open the frame file (which has the same name given to the frame in Step 6), open another photo and drag it from the Photo Bin into the frame area.

4 Click on the **Create Frame** button

5 Click on the **Save Frame** button

6 Give the frame a name and click on the **OK** button

Enter Frame Name

Please enter a name for your new frame:

Sunset

OK

Cancel

7 Click on the **Done** button to complete the Guided edit and save the frame as a new image (this should be as a PSD image)

Done

Beware

Frames that are created with the Frame Creator option are not available from the **Frames** button on the Quick edit mode bottom toolbar. They can be opened as a normal image file (if saved as a PSD file to preserve the layers), and they are also available in Expert edit mode from the **Graphics** panel button (select the **My Frames** option from the **Show All** drop-down menu).

Artistic Overlays

One of the artistic Guided edits can be used to place an artistic shape over a subject in an image and apply effects to the background and within the shape. To do this:

Artistic Overlays is a new feature in Elements 2018.

1 Open the image to which you want to add an overlay effect. Access Guided edit mode and in the **Fun Edits** section, click on the **Shape Overlay Effect** button

SHAPE OVERLAY EFFECT

Add a shape overlay effect to create an artistic look.

2 Click on the **Select a shape** button and click on a shape. The shape is placed over the image

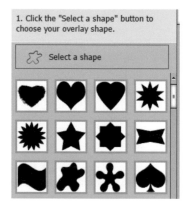

1. Click the "Select a shape" button to choose your overlay shape.

Select a shape

3 Click on the **Move Tool** button and drag the shape into position on the image

Move Tool

Click on the green tick icon to accept the position of the shape once it has been moved using the Move Tool. Click on the red circle to reject it.

4 Click on the **Outside Effect** button and select an effect for the area outside the selection shape

3. Choose an effect for the area outside of the shape.

Outside Effect

5 Click on the **Inside Effect** button and select an effect for the area inside the selection shape

4. Choose an effect for the area inside of the shape.

Inside Effect

If you do not like an effect that has been added in Step 4 or 5, click on the Undo button in the panel.

6 Click on the **Crop Tool** button to crop the image to a custom size. Click on the **Crop to Shape** button to generate a preset crop

5. (Optional) Crop your photo.

Crop Tool

Use the Crop Tool to manually crop the photo.

OR

Crop to Shape

Use Crop to Shape to automatically crop the photo.

7 The **Crop to Shape** option crops the image around the shape that was added in Step 2

8 Click on the **Next** button to complete the overlay effect and save, edit or share it as shown on page 97

The **Crop to Shape** option creates a tight crop around the overlay shape. Use the standard **Crop** tool to include more of the background.

Double Exposures

The Double Exposure Guided edit can be used to combine two photos to create a surreal effect. To do this:

Open the image to which you want to add the double exposure effect. Access Guided edit mode and in the **Fun Edits** section, click on the **Double Exposure** button

Double Exposure is a new feature in Elements 2018.

Click on the **Crop Tool** button and drag around the main subject to ensure it is in the middle of the image

Crop Tool

Click on one of the selection tools and use it to select the main subject

2. Use one of the selection tools to choose the primary subject of your photo.

Auto   Quick

Hot tip

It is best to make a reasonably large selection in Step 3, otherwise the double exposure effect of the imported photo in Step 4 may be too over-powering for the size of the selection.

Click on the **Import a photo** button, or select one of the preset photos, to superimpose it over the subject selected in the previous step

3. Choose a photo to superimpose on your primary subject.

Import a photo

OR

Forest   City   Cloud

Intensity :

Click on the **Move Tool** button to position the superimposed photo

Move Tool

Click on the **Effects** button and select an effect to be applied to the image

ƒx Effects

Click on the **Next** button to complete the effect and save, edit or share it as shown on page 97

Watercolors

Watercolors are more commonly associated with paintings, but with Guided edits, similar effects can be added to photos.

1 Open the image that you want to use to add a watercolor effect. Access Guided edit mode and in the **Special Edits** section, click on the **Watercolor Effects** button

2 Click on the watercolor effect, which will be applied to the whole image

3 Click on the **Watercolor Paper** button and click on one of the options to add this as an overlay over the whole image

4 Click on the **Canvas Texture** button and click on one of the options to add a texture effect over the whole image, to create the final watercolor effect

The Watercolor effect is a new feature in Elements 2018.

105

Hot tip

Once the **Watercolor Paper** option is applied, this changes the overall appearance of the image, by adding color to the effect selected in Step 2.

Don't forget

Text can also be added to the watercolor, using the **Type Tool** and **Type Style** buttons.

5 Click on the **Next** button to complete the watercolor effect and save, edit or share it as shown on page 97

Replacing Backgrounds

Replacing an unwanted background with something more appealing is possible in Guided edits. To do this:

The Replace Background option is a new feature in Elements 2018.

If **None** is selected in Step 3, the selected subject appears on a blank background.

If the Refine Edge Brush is not used, the main subject may not appear properly blended with the background; i.e. its edges will appear too defined and harsh.

1 Open the image containing a background that you want to replace. Access Guided edit mode and in the **Special Edits** section, click on the **Replace Background** button

Change the background of your photo.

2 Click on one of the selection tools and use it to select the main subject in the image (not the background)

1. Use one of the Selection Tools to choose the primary subject of your photo.

Auto   Quick

Brush   Refine

3 In the **Choose a new background** section click on the **Import a photo** button to select one of your own photos for the background, or click on the Presets, None or Color buttons. Select an image as required, which will become the background

2. Choose a new background

Import a photo

OR

Presets   None   Color

4 Click on the **Move Tool** button to move the main subject over the background

Move Tool

5 Click on the **Refine Edge Brush** button to smooth the edges of the main subject over the background

Refine Edge Brush

6 Click on the **Next** button to complete the Replace Background effect and save, edit or share it as shown on page 97

6 Beyond Basic Color Editing

This chapter looks at some of the more powerful features for image editing in Elements, so you can take your skills to the next level.

Hue and Saturation

The Hue/Saturation command can be used to edit the color elements of an image. However, it works slightly differently from other commands, such as those for the brightness and contrast. There are three areas that are covered by the Hue/Saturation command: color (hue), color strength (saturation) and lightness. To adjust the hue and saturation of an image:

Hot tip

The keyboard shortcut for accessing the Hue/Saturation dialog window is Ctrl + U (Command key + U on a Mac).

Hot tip

By altering the hue of an image, some interesting abstract color effects can be created. This can be very effective if you are producing several versions of the same image, such as for an artistic poster.

Don't forget

Hue is used to describe the color of a particular pixel or an image.

 Open an image

 Select **Enhance > Adjust Color > Adjust Hue/ Saturation** from the Menu bar, in either Expert or Quick edit modes

 Drag this slider to adjust the hue of the image; i.e. change the colors in the image

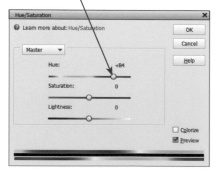

...cont'd

 Drag this slider to adjust the saturation; i.e. the intensity of colors in the image

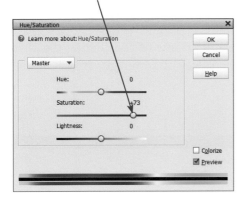

The Lightness option is similar to adjusting image brightness.

5 Check on the **Colorize** box to color the image with the hue of the currently-selected foreground color in the Color Picker, which is located at the bottom of the Toolbox

The Colorize option can be used to create some interesting "color wash" effects. Try altering the Hue slider once the Colorize box has been checked On.

6 Click on the **OK** button to apply any changes that have been made

For more on working with color and the Color Picker, see page 162.

Histogram

The Histogram in Elements is a device that displays the tonal range of the pixels in an image, and it can be used for very precise editing of an image. The Histogram (**Window** > **Histogram** in Expert edit mode) is a graph that displays how the pixels in an image are distributed across the image, from the darkest (black) to the lightest (white) points. Another way of considering the Histogram is that it displays the values of an image's highlights, midtones and shadows:

The keyboard shortcut for accessing the Histogram is F9.

The Histogram works by looking at the individual color channels of an image (Red, Green, Blue, also known as the RGB color model) or a combination of all three, which is displayed as Luminosity in the Channel box. It can also look at all of the colors in an image.

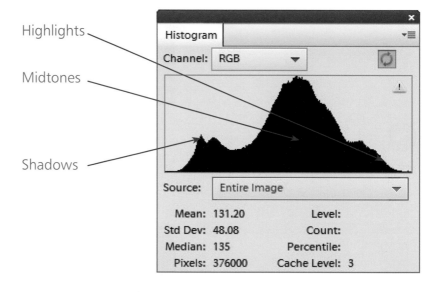

Highlights

Midtones

Shadows

110

Image formats such as JPEG are edited in Elements using the RGB color model; i.e. red, green and blue, mixed together to create the colors in the image.

Highlights

Midtones

Shadows

...cont'd

Ideally, the Histogram should show a reasonably consistent range of tonal distribution, indicating an image that has good contrast and detail:

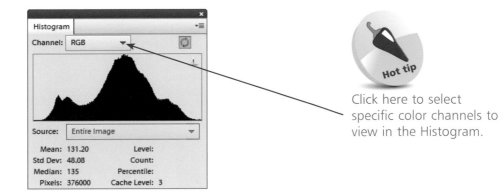

Hot tip

Click here to select specific color channels to view in the Histogram.

However, if the tonal range is bunched at one end of the graph, this indicates that the image is under-exposed or over-exposed:

Over-exposure

Hot tip

If the Histogram is left open, it will update automatically as editing changes are made to an image. This gives a good idea of how effective the changes are.

Under-exposure

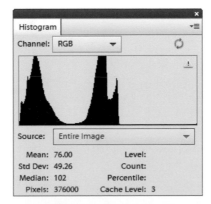

Levels

While the Histogram displays the tonal range of an image, the Levels function can be used to edit this range. Any changes made using the Levels function will then be visible in the Histogram. Levels allows you to redistribute pixels between the darkest and lightest points in an image, and also set these points manually if you want to. To use the Levels function:

Hot tip

The Levels function can be used to adjust the tonal range of a specific area of an image, by first making a selection and then using the Levels dialog box. For more details on selecting areas, see Chapter 7.

Don't forget

In the Levels dialog box, the graph is the same as the one shown in the Histogram.

Don't forget

Image shadows, midtones and highlights can be altered by dragging the markers for the black, midtone and white input points.

 Open an image

 Select **Enhance** > **Adjust Lighting** > **Levels** from the Menu bar, in either Expert or Quick edit modes

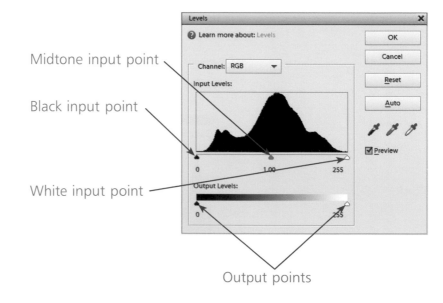

Midtone input point

Black input point

White input point

Output points

3 Drag the black point and the white point sliders to, or beyond, the first pixels denoted in the graph to increase the contrast

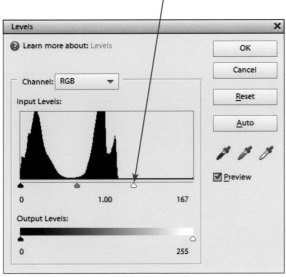

It is worth adjusting an image's black and white points before any other editing is performed.

Move the midtone point slider to darken or lighten the midtones in an image.

4 Drag the output sliders towards the middle to decrease the contrast

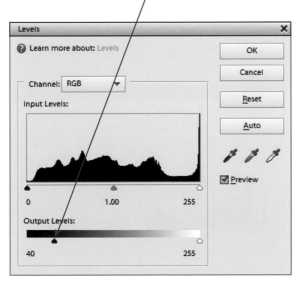

The Auto button in the Levels dialog box produces the same effect as using the **Enhance > Auto Levels** command from the Menu bar.

113

Adjustments with Levels

Although there is an Auto Levels function within Elements, more accurate editing can be done by using the Levels dialog box:

The Auto Levels option can be accessed by selecting **Enhance > Auto Levels** from the Menu bar.

The keyboard shortcut for accessing the Levels dialog window is Ctrl + L (Command key + L on a Mac).

By default, all of the color channels (RGB for Red, Green and Blue) are edited within Levels. However, click here to select the individual Red, Green and Blue channels so that they can be edited independently.

1 Open an image that is either too dark or too light (or requires the midtones to be edited)

2 Select **Enhance > Adjust Lighting > Levels** from the Menu bar

3 If there is no data at one end of the graph, it suggests an image is either too dark or too light (in this instance, too dark). Drag on this button to adjust the image

...cont'd

4 Drag the button to where the graph starts (or finishes). Ideally, the white and black buttons should be at the right and left of the graph respectively

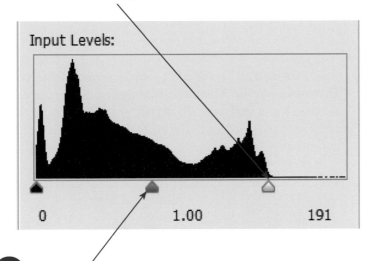

5 Drag on this button to adjust the midtones of an image; i.e. the color in the mid-range between white and black

6 The Levels editing effects are applied to the image

Hot tip

Adjusting the midtones manually is similar to using **Enhance > Adjust Lighting > Shadows/Highlights** from the Menu bar.

Don't forget

Levels can also be accessed and applied in Quick edit mode.

7 Click on the **OK** button to exit the Levels dialog window

OK

Color Curves

If the colors are not ideal in a photo, one option for editing them is with Color Curves. This is done by editing the colors for different elements in the image; e.g. highlights, brightness, contrast and shadows. This can be done with preset options, or you can apply your own settings manually. To use Color Curves:

1 Select **Enhance** > **Adjust Color** > **Adjust Color Curves** from the Menu bar. The Adjust Color Curves window has a **Before** and **After** preview panel at the top of the window, and options for automatic and manual adjustments at the bottom of the window

2 Under the **Select a Style:** heading, select the area of color that you want to edit. These include **Backlight** (for images where the foreground subject is too dark), **Darken Highlights**, **Default**, **Increase Contrast**, **Increase Midtones**, **Lighten Shadows** and **Solarize**

3 For each item selected in Step 2, the appropriate curve adjustments are made automatically (shown on the graph)

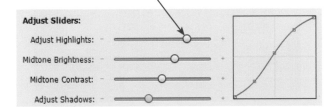

4 Drag the sliders under **Adjust Sliders:** to edit the color elements in the image manually. As you drag the sliders, the graph moves accordingly

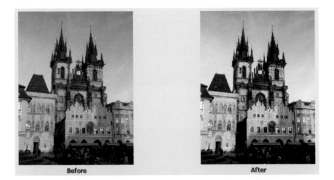

Dragging the sliders in Step 4 is a good way to see how the shape of the Color Curves graph affects the image.

117

5 The Color Curves editing effects are previewed at the top of the window

Before   After

Exaggerated colors created with curves can make a striking photo, even if it is not completely realistic.

6 Click on the **OK** button to apply the changes, **Cancel** to remove them, or **Reset** to return to the original image and continue editing it

OK

Cancel

Reset

Remove Color Cast

Even sophisticated digital cameras and smartphone cameras can sometimes misinterpret the lighting conditions of a scene, resulting in an unnatural color in the photo, known as color cast. To remove this:

Don't forget

There is no keyboard shortcut for accessing the Remove Color Cast dialog window.

Don't forget

Color cast is particularly common in indoor shots taken without the flash under artificial lighting. This is known as "white balance", where the camera does not correctly interpret what white should be, and so all of the other colors in the photo are affected too. One way to overcome this is to change your camera's white balance settings if you are taking photos in artificial lighting.

Hot tip

Color cast can be edited manually within Levels. To do this, select one of the individual color channels (Red, Green or Blue) in the Levels dialog window and drag the input sliders accordingly.

 In Expert or Quick edit modes, open the photo affected by color cast

2 Select **Enhance > Adjust Color > Remove Color Cast** from the Menu bar. Click on an area of the photo that should be black, white or gray. The overall color in the photo will be adjusted accordingly

7

Working with Selections

The true power of digital image editing comes into its own when you are able to select areas of an image and edit them independently.

This chapter looks at the various ways that selections can be made and edited, using the tools and functions within Elements.

About Selections

One of the most important aspects of image editing is the ability to select areas within an image. This can be used in a number of different ways:

- Selecting an object to apply an editing technique to it (such as changing the brightness or contrast) without affecting the rest of the image.

- Selecting a particular color in an image.

- Selecting an area on which to apply a special effect.

- Selecting an area to remove.

Expert edit mode has several tools that can be used to select items, and there are also a number of editing functions that can be applied to selections.

Two examples of how selections can be used are:

Don't forget

Once a selection has been made, it stays selected even when another tool is activated, to allow further editing to take place.

Don't forget

If a selection is deleted, the space will be filled by the current background color in the Color Picker in the Toolbox.

Hot tip

The best way to deselect a selection is to click on it once with one of the selection tools, preferably the one used to make the selection. You can also choose **Select** > **Deselect** from the Menu bar.

 1 Select an area within an image and delete it

 2 Select an area in an image and add a color or special effect

Marquee Tools

There are two options for the Marquee tool: the Rectangular Marquee tool and the Elliptical Marquee tool. Both of these can be used to make symmetrical selections. To use the Marquee tools:

1 Select either the **Rectangular** or the **Elliptical Marquee** tool from the Toolbox. Select the required options from the Tool Options bar

To access additional tools from the Expert edit mode Toolbox, click on a tool and select any grouped tools in the Tool Options bar.

2 Make a symmetrical selection with one of the tools by clicking and dragging on an image

Elliptical selection

To make a selection that is exactly square or round, hold down **Shift** when dragging with the Rectangular Marquee tool or the Elliptical Marquee tool respectively.

Rectangular selection

Lasso Tools

There are three options for the Lasso tool, which can be used to make freehand selections. To use these:

Lasso tool

When a selection has been completed (i.e. its end point reaches its start point), a small circle will appear at the side of whichever Lasso tool is being used. Click on this point to complete the selection.

See page 148 for information about Anti-aliasing.

1 Select the **Lasso** tool from the Toolbox and select the required options from the Tool Options bar

2 Make a freehand selection by clicking with the mouse and dragging around the object

With the Lasso tool, do not release the mouse until the selection has been completed.

Polygonal Lasso tool

1 Select the **Polygonal Lasso** tool from the Toolbox and select the required options from the Tool Options bar

2 Make a selection by clicking on specific points around an object, and then dragging to the next point

Making a selection with the Polygonal Lasso tool is like creating a dot-to-dot pattern.

Magnetic Lasso tool

1 Select the **Magnetic Lasso** tool from the Toolbox and select the required options from the Tool Options bar

2 Click once on an image to create the first anchor point

In the Tool Options bar for the Magnetic Lasso tool, the Contrast value determines the amount of contrast there has to be between colors for the selection line to snap to them. A high value detects lines with a high contrast, and vice versa.

3 Make a selection by dragging continuously around an object. The selection line snaps to the closest, strongest edge; i.e. the one with the most contrast. Fastening points are added as the selection is made

The Frequency setting in the Tool Options bar determines how quickly the fastening points are inserted as a selection is being made. A high value places the fastening points more quickly than a low value.

Magic Wand Tool

The Magic Wand tool can be used to select areas of the same or similar color. To do this:

In the Tool Options bar for the Magic Wand tool, the Tolerance box determines the range of colors that will be selected in relation to the color you click on. A low value will only select a very narrow range of colors in relation to the initially-selected one, while a high value will include a greater range. The values range from 0-255.

 Select the **Magic Wand** tool from the Toolbox and select the required options from the Tool Options bar

Magic Wand | New | Tolerance: 32 | Sample All Layers | Contiguous | Anti-aliasing | Refine Edge...

 Click on a color to select all of the adjacent pixels that are the same or similar color, depending on the options selected from the Tool Options bar

In the Tool Options bar for the Magic Wand tool, check on the **Contiguous** box to ensure that only adjacent colors are selected. To select the same or similar color throughout the image, whether adjacent or not, uncheck the Contiguous box.

Selection Brush Tool

The Selection Brush tool can be used to select areas by using a brush-like stroke. Unlike with the Marquee or Lasso tools, the area selected by the Selection Brush tool is the one directly below where the tool moves. To make a selection with the Selection Brush tool (this is also available in Quick edit mode):

 Select the **Selection Brush** tool from the Toolbox and select the required options from the Tool Options bar

The Selection Brush tool can be used to select an area, or to mask an area. This can be determined in the Selection drop-down box in the Tool Options bar.

Click and drag to make a selection

The Selection Brush tool is best for selecting large areas that do not have to be too precise. For exact precision, use the Polygonal or Magnetic Lasso tools.

For all of the selection tools, hold down Shift to make another selection while retaining the original one.

 The selection area is within the borders marked out by the Selection Brush tool

Quick Selection Tool

The Quick Selection tool can be used to select areas of similar color by drawing over the general area, without having to make a specific selection. To do this:

The Quick Selection tool is also available from the Quick edit mode Toolbox.

Beware

If a very large brush size is used for the Quick Selection tool – e.g. 300 px (pixels) or above – you may select unwanted areas of the image by mistake.

Don't forget

As you drag the Quick Selection tool, it selects whichever areas of color it passes over. As you drag over different areas of color, these will be selected too.

1 Select the **Quick Selection** tool from the Toolbox

2 Select the required options from the Tool Options bar

3 Draw over an area, or part of an area, to select all of the similarly-colored pixels

Smart Brush Tool

The Smart Brush tool can be used to quickly select large areas in an image (in a similar way to the Quick Selection tool) and then have effects applied automatically to the selected area. To do this:

 1 Open the image to which you want to apply changes

127

 2 Select the **Smart Brush** tool from the Toolbox

 3 Select the editing effect you want to apply to the area selected by the Smart Brush tool, from the Tool Options bar

4 Select **Brush size** for the Smart Brush tool, from the Tool Options bar

5 Drag the Smart Brush tool over an area of the image. In the left-hand image below, the building has been selected and brightened; in the right-hand image, the sky has been selected and enhanced

Auto Selections

Instead of having to make precise selections, Elements 2018 has a function where selections can be made by dragging around a subject. Elements can then identify the subject and select it.

 1 Open an image and select the **Auto Selection** tool (from the selection tools subset)

Once a selection has been made, it can be inverted by choosing **Select** > **Inverse** from the Menu bar. The keyboard shortcut for inverting a selection is Shift + Ctrl + I (Shift + Command key + I on a Mac).

2 Drag the **Auto Selection** tool around the required subject. This creates a rectangular box

3 Release the **Auto Selection** tool to enable it to create the selection

When a selection has been inverted, the newly-selected area can be edited in the same way as for a standard selection in a photo.

4 Once a selection has been made in this way it can be edited independently from the rest of the image. Also, if the selection is inverted (see tip) the background can be edited and the originally-selected subject remains untouched

Feathering

Feathering is a technique that can be used to soften the edges of a selection by making them slightly blurry. This can be used if you are pasting a selection into another image, or if you want to soften the edges around a portrait of an individual. To do this:

1 Make a selection

2 Choose **Select** > **Feather** from the Menu bar

The keyboard shortcut for accessing the Feather Selection dialog window is Alt + Ctrl + D (Alt + Command key + D on a Mac).

3 Enter a Feather Radius value (the number of pixels wide around the radius of the selection that will be blurred). Click on the **OK** button

Feather Selection	✕
❓ Learn more about: Feather Selection	OK
	Cancel
Feather Radius: 5 pixels	

Feathering can also be selected from the Tool Options bar once a Marquee tool is selected, and before the selection has been made.

4 Invert the selection, as shown on the previous page, and delete the background by pressing **Delete** on the keyboard. This will leave the selection around the subject with softened edges

If required, crop the final image so that the feathered subject is more prominent.

Refining Selections

When making selections it is sometimes difficult to exactly select the area that you want. In Elements 2018 it is possible to refine the area of a selection, and also the edges around a selected item. To do this:

The **Refine Selection Brush** option can be used regardless of how the selection was made.

Click inside a selection to add to it; click outside to subtract from it.

1 In Expert or Quick edit mode, make a selection with one of the selection tools

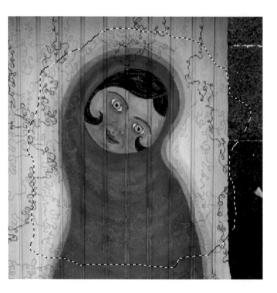

2 Select the **Refine Selection Brush** tool (grouped with the Quick Selection tool)

3 Click on this button to add or subtract from the selection with the cursor

4 Click on this button to smooth the edges of the selection by dragging the cursor over it

Click on the **View** box to select an option for the overlay that covers the current selection, so that you can see exactly what has been selected.

5 Select a size for the cursor to refine the selection, and the strength for how it snaps to neighboring pixels; the greater the strength, the more the selection will snap to pixels of similar color

...cont'd

6 Position the cursor inside or outside the selection. It appears as two circles: a smaller one inside a larger one. Use the circles to nudge the selection lines one way or another to refine the selection

Zoom in on a selection for the greatest accuracy in refining it.

Refining edges

It is also possible to add a range of refinements to the edges of a selection, which can be an excellent option for textures such as clothing or animal fur. To do this:

1 Once a selection has been made, click on the **Refine Edge...** button in the Tool Options bar

Refine Edge...

2 Select options here for how much of the edge is detected in terms of being refined. Select **Smart Radius** or enter a manual value for the radius

3 Select options here for how the edge is adjusted, using smoothing, feathering, contrast and moving the edge. Click **OK**

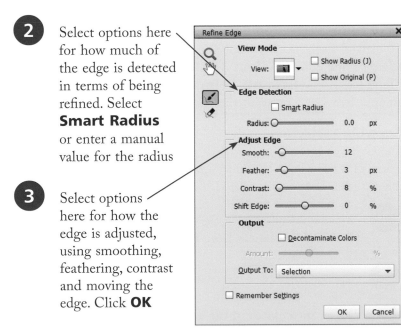

The Refine Edge options are particularly useful if you are copying a selection and pasting it into another image that has different textures.

Beware

Once an area has been moved and deselected, it cannot then be selected independently again, unless it has been copied and pasted onto a separate layer.

Hot tip

Selections can also be deselected by clicking on **Select** > **Deselect** from the Menu bar, or using Ctrl + D on the keyboard (Command key + D on a Mac).

Editing Selections

When you have made a selection you can edit it in a number of ways:

Moving a selection
Make a selection and select the **Move** tool from the Toolbox. Drag the selection to move it to a new location.

Changing the selection area
Make a selection with a selection tool. With the same tool selected, click and drag within the selection area to move it over another part of the image.

Adding to a selection
Make a selection and click on this button in the Tool Options bar. Make another selection to create a single, larger selection. The two selections do not have to intersect.

Intersecting with a selection
To create a selection by intersecting two existing selections, make a selection and click on this button in the Tool Options bar. Make another selection that intersects the first. The intersected area will become the selection.

Expanding a selection
To expand a selection by a specific number of pixels, make a selection and choose **Select** > **Modify** > **Expand** from the Menu bar. In the **Expand Selection** dialog box, enter the amount by which you want the selection expanded.

Growing a selection
The Grow command can be used on a selection when it has been made with the Magic Wand tool, and some of the pixels within the selection have been omitted. To do this:

 Make a selection with the **Magic Wand** tool and make the required choices from the Tool Options bar

 Choose **Select** > **Grow** from the Menu bar

Depending on the choices in the Tool Options bar, the omitted pixels will be included in the selection.

8 Layers

Layers provide the means to add numerous elements to an image, and edit them independently from one another. This chapter looks at how to use layers to add content to photos, and shows how to interact with layers.

Layering Images

Layering is a technique that enables you to add additional elements to an image, and place them on separate layers so that they can be edited and manipulated independently from other elements in the image. It is like creating an image using transparent sheets of film: each layer is independent of the others, but when they are combined, a composite image is created. This is an extremely versatile technique for working with digital images.

By using layers, several different elements can be combined to create a composite image:

Original image

Layers should usually be used when you are adding content to an image, as this gives more flexibility for working with the various image elements once they have been added.

Final image
With text, gradient and shapes added (four additional layers have been added).

Text and shapes cannot be added together on the same layer.

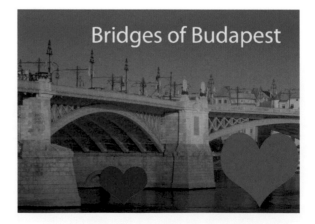

Bridges of Budapest

Layers Panel

The use of layers within Elements is done within Expert edit mode and is governed by the Layers panel. When an image is first opened it is shown in the Layers panel as the Background layer. While this remains as the Background layer, it cannot be moved above any other layers. However, it can be converted into a normal layer, in which case it operates in the same way as any other layer. To convert a Background layer into a normal one:

The keyboard shortcut for accessing the Layers panel is F11.

1 Click on the **Layers** button on the Taskbar

2 The open image is shown in the Layers panel as the Background

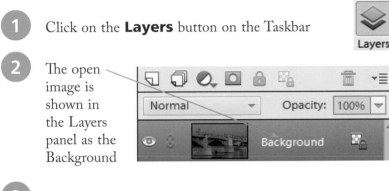

The Background layer can also be converted into a normal one by applying the Background Eraser tool and the Magic Eraser tool.

3 Double-click on the layer. Enter a name for it and click on the **OK** button

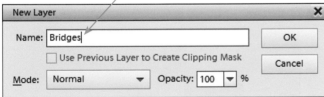

4 The Background layer is converted into a normal layer in the Layers panel

The Layers panel menu can be accessed from the button in the top right-hand corner of the Layers panel.

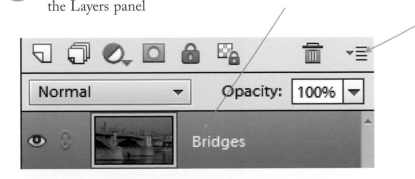

135

Adding Layers

New blank layers can be added whenever you want to include new content within an image. This could be part of another image that has been copied and pasted; a whole new image; some text; or an object. To add a new layer:

The keyboard shortcut for adding a new layer is Shift + Ctrl + N (Shift + Command key + N on a Mac).

1 Click here on the Layers panel

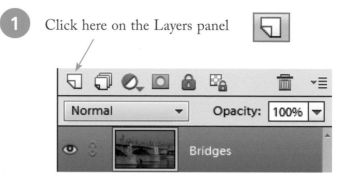

Don't forget

Text is automatically added on a new layer within an image.

2 Double-click on the layer name and overtype to give the layer a new name

Don't forget

To edit an item on a particular layer, first make sure that the correct layer is selected in the Layers panel. A selected layer is known as the active layer and it is highlighted in the Layers panel with a solid color around it.

3 With the new layer selected in the Layers panel, add content to this layer. This will be visible over the layer, or layers, below it

Fill and Adjustment Layers

Fill and Adjustment layers can be added to images to give an effect behind or above the main subject. To do this:

 Open the Layers panel and select a layer. The Fill or Adjustment layer will be placed directly above the selected layer

 Click here at the bottom of the Layers panel

3 Select one of the Fill or Adjustment options. The Fill options are **Solid Color...**, **Gradient...** or **Pattern...**

Solid Color...
Gradient...
Pattern...

Levels...
Brightness/Contrast...

Hue/Saturation...
Gradient Map...
Photo Filter...

Invert
Threshold...
Posterize...

For a Fill layer to be visible behind the main image, the image must have a transparent background. To achieve this, select the main subject. Choose **Select** > **Inverse** from the Menu bar and press the **Delete** key to delete the background. A checkerboard effect should be visible, which denotes that this part of the image is transparent. This only works on layers that have been converted into normal layers, rather than the Background one.

The Adjustments panel is also used for Levels, Brightness/Contrast, Hue/Saturation, Gradient Map, Photo Filter, Threshold and Posterize.

...cont'd

Hot tip

Fill and Adjustment layers can also be added from the Layer option on the Menu bar.

Hot tip

If you want to edit a Fill or Adjustment layer, double-click on its icon in the Layers panel and then apply the required changes.

Beware

If the opacity for a Fill layer is 100%, nothing will be visible beneath that layer.

4 For a Solid Color, Gradient or Pattern Fill, the required Fill is selected from the dialog box and this is added to the selected layer

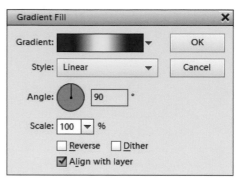

5 For Adjustment options, settings can be applied within the Adjustments panel

6 Once Fill and Adjustment settings have been applied, the effect can be edited by changing the opacity. This is done by dragging this slider, which appears when the Opacity box is clicked On

7 The opacity level determines how much of the image is visible through the Fill or Adjustment layer

Working with Layers

Moving layers

The order in which layers are arranged in the Layers panel is known as the stacking order. It is possible to change a layer's position in the stacking order, which affects how it is viewed in the composite image. To do this:

1 Click and drag a layer within the Layers panel to change its stacking order

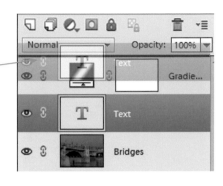

Hiding layers

Layers can be hidden while you are working on other parts of an image. However, the layer is still part of the composite image – it has not been removed. To hide a layer:

1 Click here so that a line appears through the eye icon, and the layer becomes hidden. Click again to remove the line and reveal the layer

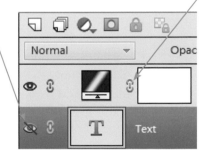

Locking layers

Layers can be locked, so that they cannot be edited accidentally while you are working on other parts of an image. To do this:

1 Select a layer and click here so that the padlock is activated. The padlock also appears on the layer itself

Beware

Layers cannot be moved underneath the Background layer, unless it has been renamed.

Don't forget

This icon indicates that the layer has a layer mask linked to it. This means that the mask will move with the layer, if it is moved. Click on the icon to unlink the layer mask from the layer (see pages 142-144 for details about layer masks).

Beware

Layers can be deleted by selecting them and clicking on the **Trash** icon in the Layers panel. However, this also deletes all of the content on that layer.

Grouping Layers

When working with layers it can become rather confusing when there are a large number associated with one image. For instance, if a lot of layer effects have been added, it can be hard to work out which layer is which. To simplify this, layers in Elements 2018 can be grouped together and color coded, so that layers with the same effects can be contained within one group heading. To use grouped layers:

Hot tip

Layers can also be added to a group once they have had effects or content added to them.

Beware

Layers cannot be added to a group by selecting a group in the Layers panel and then creating a new layer. In this case, the new layer will be outside the group.

1 Click here on the Layers panel to create a group

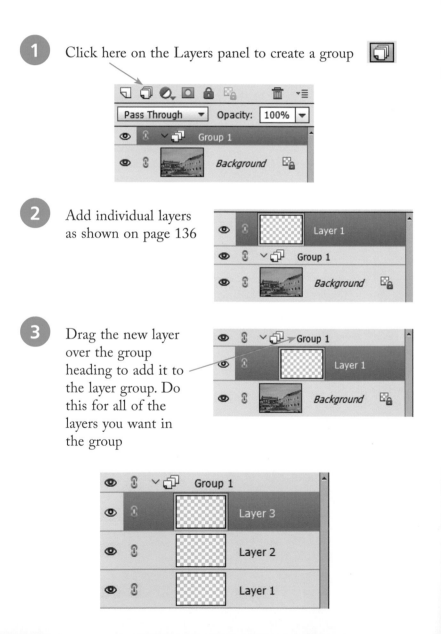

2 Add individual layers as shown on page 136

3 Drag the new layer over the group heading to add it to the layer group. Do this for all of the layers you want in the group

4 Add the required effects or content to the layers in the group; e.g. create a group containing different text layers within the image

Double-click on the group name to highlight it so that it can be renamed (or right-click on the group name and click on the **Rename** button).

5 Right-click on a group name and select a color for the group (this is also displayed on all of the group layers)

No Color
Red
Orange
Yellow
Green
Blue
Violet
Gray

Individual layers can also be color coded, in the same way as for groups.

6 Click on this button to minimize a group (the layers remain active within the group)

The selections made in Step 7 will be applied to all of the layers within the group.

7 Click here to determine how the group layer interacts with the layers below it, and its level of opacity

Layer Masks

Because layers can be separated within an individual image, there is a certain amount of versatility in terms of the ways in which different layers can interact with each other. One of these ways is to create a Layer Mask. This is a top-level layer, through which an area is removed so that the layer below is revealed. To do this:

Beware

If the Background layer is not renamed as in Step 2, the graphic will be placed directly over the Background layer, rather than being created on a new layer.

Don't forget

When creating the new layer in Step 2, you can also change the opacity and select a different mode, to affect the way the layer interacts with layers below it (if there are any).

Don't forget

Different types of content can be added as the top layer in an image to be used as a Layer Mask, although whatever is added has to be converted to a normal layer rather than a background one.

1 Open an image. It will be displayed as the Background in the Layers panel. Double-click on this to select it

2 Give the layer a new name and click on the **OK** button

3 Click on the **Graphics** button on the Taskbar to access the Graphics panel

4 Use the drop-down menus at the top of the Graphics panel to access different categories and click on a graphic to select it

5 Select a graphic and double-click on it to add it as a layer to the current image.

Initially, this is added below the open image. Rename the new layer

Don't forget

If a new layer is not renamed, it will automatically become the Background one.

6 Drag the added layer above the original image (this can also be done by selecting an area in

another image, copying it and then pasting it above the existing image)

7 The graphic image layer now covers the original one

Beware

The top layer will obscure all layers below it, until either its opacity is reduced, or a Layer Mask is applied.

...cont'd

Don't forget

If the Brush tool is used to create the Layer Mask, this is done by drawing over the top layer of the image. As this is done, the layer below will be revealed. Change the level of opacity in the Tool Options bar to change the amount that the layer below shows through the top layer of the image.

Don't forget

The selected layer can also be deleted by pressing the **Delete** key on the keyboard.

Hot tip

Build up an image with several Layer Masks, to create an artistic effect.

8 Click here to apply a layer mask to the top layer

9 Select either one of the **Marquee** tools, the **Lasso** tools, or the **Brush** tool from the Toolbox

10 Select an area on the top layer and delete it, to display the image below it (**Edit** > **Delete** from the Menu bar)

11 In the Layers panel, the area that has been removed is displayed here

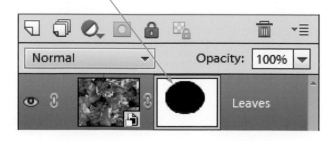

Opacity

The opacity of a layer can be set to determine how much of the layer below is visible through the selected layer. To do this:

1 Select a layer either in the Layers panel or by clicking on the relevant item within an image

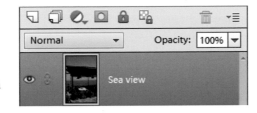

2 Click here and drag the slider that appears below, to achieve the required level of opacity. The greater the amount of opacity, the less transparent the selected layer becomes

3 The opacity setting determines how much of the background or the layer below is visible through the selected one. This can be used to create some interesting artistic effects, including a watermark effect if the opacity is applied to a single layer with nothing behind it

Hot tip

The background behind an image to which opacity has been applied can be changed within the Preferences section. Select **Edit > Preferences** from the Menu bar (**Adobe Photoshop Elements Editor > Preferences** on a Mac) and then select **Transparency** and edit the items in the Grid Colors box.

Don't forget

Different layers can have different levels of opacity applied to them.

Saving Layers

Once an image has been created using two or more layers, there are two ways in which the composite image can be saved: in a proprietary Photoshop format, in which case individual layers are maintained; or in a general file format, where all of the layers will be merged into a single one. The advantage of the former is that individual elements can still be edited within the image, independently of other items. In general, it is good practice to save layered images in both a Photoshop and a non-Photoshop format. To save layered images in a Photoshop format:

1 Select **File** > **Save As** from the Menu bar

2 Make sure Photoshop (*.PSD, *.PDD) is selected as the format

3 Make sure the Layers box is checked On

4 Click on the **Save** button

To save in a non-Photoshop format, select **File** > **Save As** from the Menu bar. Select the file format from the Format box (such as JPEG or TIFF) and click on the **Save** button. The Layers box will not be available.

Beware

Layered images that are saved in the Photoshop PSD/PDD format can increase dramatically in file size, compared with the original image or a layered image that has been flattened.

9 Text and Drawing Tools

Elements has options for adding and formatting text, and creating a variety of graphical objects. This chapter looks at how to add and manipulate text and drawing objects.

Adding and Formatting Text

Text can be added to images in Elements and this can be used to create a wide range of items such as cards, brochures and posters. To add text to an image:

Beware

Use the Vertical Type tool sparingly, as this is not a natural way for the eye to read text. Use it with small amounts of text, for effect.

148

Don't forget

Anti-aliasing is a technique that smoothes out the jagged edges that can sometimes appear with text when viewed on a computer monitor. Anti-aliasing is created by adding pixels to the edges of text, so that it blends more smoothly with the background.

1 Select the **Horizontal** or **Vertical Type** tool from the Toolbox

2 Drag on the image with the Type tool to create a text box

3 Make the required formatting selections from the Tool Options bar:

Type tools   Font type   Font size

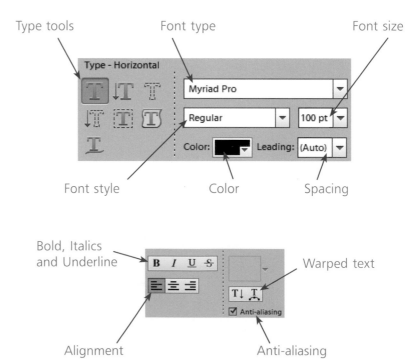

Font style   Color   Spacing

Bold, Italics and Underline   Warped text

Alignment   Anti-aliasing

4 Type the text onto the image. This is automatically placed onto the image as a new layer, at the top of the stacking order in the Layers panel

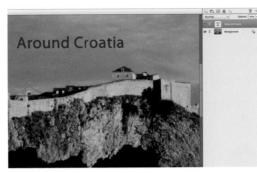

Each new text box is placed on a new layer.

5 To move the text, select it with the **Move** tool, then click and drag it to a new position

If there are two or more text layers, they can be moved above or below each other in the Layers panel.

To format text that has already been entered:

1 Select a **Type** tool and drag it over a piece of text to select it

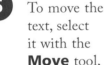

2 Make the changes in the Tool Options bar, as shown in Step 3 on the previous page

3 Click on the green check mark to accept the text entry

Individual words can be selected by double-clicking on them. Text blocks without any returns in the text can be selected by triple-clicking on them. Text blocks containing returns in the text can be selected by quadruple-clicking on them.

Customizing Text

As well as adding standard text, it is also possible to add text to follow a selection, a shape or a custom path. This can be done within Expert edit and Quick edit modes.

Adding text to a selection
To add text to a selection within an image:

Don't forget

In Expert edit mode, select the Move tool and click and drag the text to move it with the selection area.

150

Click on the **Type** tool and select the **Text on Selection** tool option

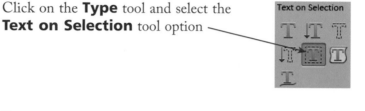

Drag over an area of an image to make a selection

Click on the green check mark to accept the selection

Hot tip

Text on Selection text should be reasonably large in size, so that it can be read clearly on the image.

Click anywhere on the selection and add text. By default, this will be displayed along the outside of the selection

Format the text in the same way as with standard text

Adding text to a shape
To add text to a shape within an image:

1 Click on the **Type** tool and select the **Text on Shape** tool option

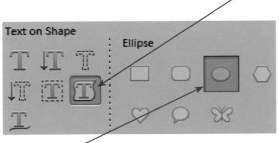

2 Click here in the Tool Options bar to select a shape

3 Drag over an area of an image to create a shape

4 Click anywhere on the shape and add text. Click on the green check mark as in Step 3 on the previous page

5 Format the text in the same way as with standard text

Beware

The butterfly shape is an artistic one, but it can be difficult reading text that is added in this way.

Hot tip

Once customized text has been added and accepted, it can still be edited in the same way as standard text, by using the Horizontal Type Tool and selecting the customized text.

Beware

Make sure that there is a good contrast between the text color and the background colors in the image.

...cont'd

Adding text to a custom path

Text can also be added to a custom path that you draw onto an image. To do this:

The Modify button in Step 2 is used to edit an existing text path. See the next page for more information.

1 Open the image onto which you want to create text on a custom path

Hot tip

If there are natural contours in an image, these can be used for the custom path.

2 Click on the **Type** tool and select the **Text on Path** tool option. Make sure the **Draw** button is also selected

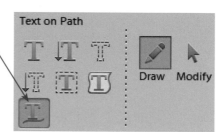

Text on Path

Draw   Modify

3 Draw a custom path on the image

Don't forget

More than one text path can be added to an image, if required.

4 Click on the green check mark to accept the text path

5 Click anywhere on the custom path and add text

Beware

Always check the spelling when adding text to a custom path, or any other text in an image.

6 Format the text in the same way as with standard text

Don't forget

Double-click on the text on a text path to select it and edit it, if required.

7 Click on the **Modify** tool in the Tool Options bar. This activates the markers along the custom path

8 Drag the markers to move the position of the custom path

Beware

If there is too much text on a custom path it can become jumbled, particularly if you adjust the markers on the path.

9 The custom path can be used to position text in a variety of ways around objects or people

153

Distorting Text

In addition to producing standard text, it is also possible to create some dramatic effects by distorting text. To do this:

Hot tip

It is possible to select the distort options once a text tool has been selected but before the text is added.

Beware

Use text distortion sparingly, as it can become annoying if it is overdone.

Don't forget

Warped text does not change the font, size or color of the existing text. However, this can be done after the effect has been applied, by double-clicking on the text.

 Enter plain text and select it by dragging a **Type** tool over it

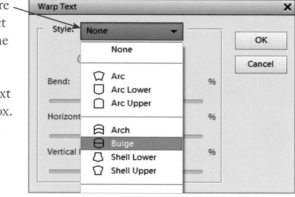

 Click the **Create Warped Text** button on the Tool Options bar

 Click here and select one of the options in the Warp Text dialog box. Click on the **OK** button

Warp Text	✕
Style: None ▼	OK
	Cancel
None	
Bend: Arc	%
Arc Lower	
Arc Upper	
Horizont Arch	%
Bulge	
Vertical Shell Lower	%
Shell Upper	

④ The selected effect is applied to the text

Text and Shape Masks

Text Masks can be used to reveal an area of an image showing through the text. This can be used to produce eye-catching headings and slogans. To do this:

 Select the **Horizontal** or **Vertical Type Mask** tool from the Toolbox

Text Mask effects work best if the text used is fairly large in size. In some cases it is a good idea to use bold text, as this is wider than standard text.

2 Click on an image, then enter and format text as you would for normal text. A red mask is applied to the image when the mask text is entered

Text and Shape Masks are always red and do not show in the final image.

3 Press **Enter** or click the **Move** tool to border the mask text with dots

A range of shapes can be added to an image from the Custom Shape tool in the Toolbox.

...cont'd

Text Masks can also be moved around in the original image, using the **Move** tool.

4 Select **Edit** > **Copy** from the Menu bar

5 Select **File** > **New** from the Menu bar and create a new file

6 Select **Edit** > **Paste** from the Menu bar to paste the Text Mask into the new file

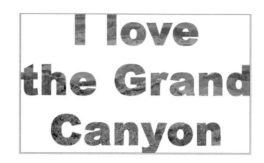

Hot tip

Once a Text Mask has been copied, it can also be pasted into other types of documents such as Word and desktop publishing documents.

Cookie Cutter masks

A similar effect can be created with Shape Masks by using the Cookie Cutter tool (grouped with the Crop tool):

1 Select the **Cookie Cutter** tool in the Toolbox and click here to select a particular style in the Tool Options bar

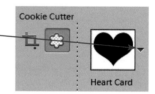

2 Drag on an image to create a cut-out effect

Don't forget

The Cookie Cutter shapes have several different categories that can be selected from the **Shapes** box above the current shapes. The categories include: Animals, Flowers, Music, Nature, Ornaments, Signs, and Talk Bubbles.

Paint Bucket Tool

The Paint Bucket tool can be used to add a solid color to a selection or an area in an image. To do this:

1 Open the image to which you want to apply the solid color using the Paint Bucket tool

For more information on working with color, see page 162.

2 Select the **Paint Bucket** tool from the Toolbox (the foreground color is selected by default)

The Paint Bucket tool can also be loaded with a pattern.

3 Select the **Opacity** and **Tolerance** in the Tool Options bar. The Tolerance determines how much of an image is affected by the Paint Bucket

The higher the tolerance, the greater the area of color applied with the Paint Bucket tool.

4 Click once on an area of solid color with the Paint Bucket tool. The color specified in Step 2 will be applied

Make a selection on an image and then apply the Paint Bucket tool to it, to get the color added exactly where you want.

Gradient Tool

The Gradient tool can be used to add a Gradient Fill to a selection in an image, or to an entire image. To do this:

1 Select an area in an image or select an object

2 Select the **Gradient** tool from the Toolbox

3 Click here in the Tool Options bar to select preset Gradient Fills

4 Click on a Gradient style to apply it as the default

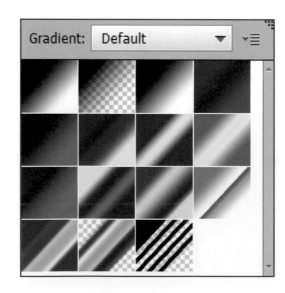

...cont'd

5 Click here in the Tool Options bar to access the **Gradient Editor** dialog box

Hot tip

To create a new preset Gradient, create it in the Gradient Editor dialog box and click on the **Add to Preset** button, to add it to the list of preset Gradients. Click on the Gradient's icon to give it a unique name in the **Name** box.

6 Click and drag the sliders to change the amount of a particular color in the Gradient

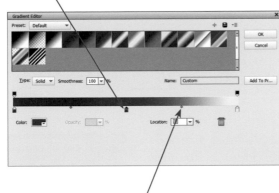

Don't forget

The more color markers that are added in Step 7, the more complex the final Gradient will be.

159

7 Click along here to add a new color marker. Click on the **OK** button

8 Click an icon in the Tool Options bar to select a Gradient style

9 Click and drag within the original selection to specify the start and end points of the Gradient effect

Don't forget

The amount that the cursor is dragged when adding a Gradient determines where the centerpoint of the Gradient is located, and also the size of each segment of the Gradient.

Brush Tool Settings

The Brush tool is very versatile and can be used to create lines of varying thickness and style. There are numerous settings that can be applied, for different styles and effects. To use this:

It is also possible to create your own brush styles, based on part of a photo. To do this, in Expert edit mode make a selection on a photo and select **Edit > Define Brush from Selection** from the Menu bar. Enter a name in the **Brush Name** dialog box and click **OK**. The customized brush is added to the Brush box in Step 3 and can be used to draw on a photo. This operates more like a stamp than a brush. Click once to add the brush image to a photo.

 Select the **Brush** tool from the Toolbox. The options are shown in the Tool Options bar

 Click here to select a default brush style

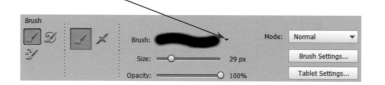

 Select a brush size and style (Hard or Rounded edges) or scroll through the **Brush** box to select different brush styles

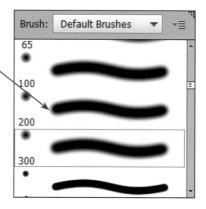

Change the **Opacity** setting for the brush in the Tool Options bar to alter the amount of background that is visible behind a brush stroke, including the Define Brush style, above.

 Click here to select a different brush type

5 Select a size and style for the brush selected in Step 4

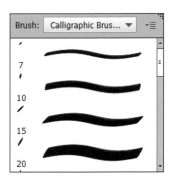

6 Click on the **Brush Settings...** button in Step 2 to make selections for the appearance of the brush

Brush Settings...

7 Drag these sliders to apply the settings for each brush type

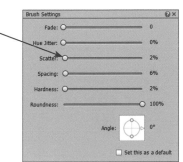

Here are some examples:

- From top to bottom: default brushes with hard edges, rounded edges and 50% opacity applied.

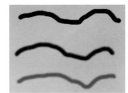

- From top to bottom: default brushes with **Scatter** applied at 50% and **Hue Jitter** at 50%.

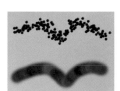

- From top to bottom: the **Calligraphic Brush** and the **Special Effects Brush (Drippy Watercolor)**.

Beware

Always check the foreground and background colors before you add any colors to an image, to ensure you have the right ones.

Hot tip

Whenever the foreground or background color squares are clicked on, the Color Picker tool is automatically activated. This can be used to select a color from anywhere on the screen.

Don't forget

The Color Swatches panel can be used to access different color panels that can be used to select the foreground and background colors. To do this: select **Window** > **Color Swatches** from the Menu bar and click on a color to select it.

Working with Color

All of the text and drawing tools make extensive use of color. Elements provides a number of methods for selecting colors, and also for working with them.

Foreground and background colors

At the bottom of the Toolbox there are two colored squares. These represent the currently-selected foreground and background colors. The foreground color, which is the most frequently used, is the one that is applied to drawing objects, such as fills and lines, and also text. The background color is used for items such as Gradient Fills, and for areas that have been removed with the Eraser tool.

Foreground color   Swap foreground and background colors

Set foreground to black and background to white

Background color

Color Picker

The Color Picker can be used to select a new color for the foreground or background color. To do this:

1   Click once on the foreground or the background color square, as required

2   In the Color Picker, click to select a color

3   Click on the **OK** button

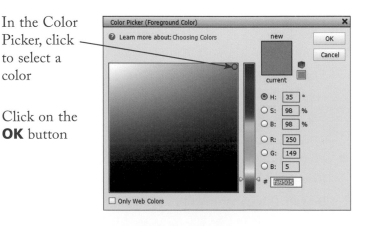

10 Becoming an Elements Expert

This chapter looks at some of the more advanced areas of Elements. These include working with the RAW file format, editing groups of images, creating catalogs and resizing images.

Importing RAW Images

RAW images are those in which the digital data has not been processed in any way, or converted into any specific file format by the camera when they were captured. These produce high quality images and are usually available on higher specification digital cameras. However, RAW is becoming more common in consumer digital cameras and RAW images can be downloaded into Elements in the same way as any other image. Once the RAW images are accessed, the Camera Raw dialog box opens so that a variety of editing functions can be applied to the image. RAW images act as a digital negative and have to be saved into another format before they can be used in the conventional way. To edit RAW images:

Don't forget

The RAW format should be used if you want to make manual changes to an image to achieve the highest possible quality.

1. Open a RAW image in the Editor or from the Organizer

2. In the Camera Raw dialog box, editing functions that are usually performed when an image is captured can be made manually

Beware

RAW images are much larger in file size than the same versions captured as JPEGs.

3. Click here to adjust the White Balance in the image

4. Drag these sliders to adjust the Color Temperature and Tint in the image

Hot tip

All images can be opened in RAW by using the **File > Open in Camera Raw** command from the Menu bar.

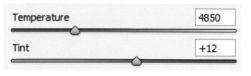

5 Drag these sliders to adjust the Exposure, Contrast, Highlights, Shadows, Whites and Blacks in the image

Auto   Default

Exposure	0.00
Contrast	0
Highlights	0
Shadows	0
Whites	0
Blacks	0

6 Click on the **Detail** tab and drag these sliders to adjust the Sharpness and Noise in the image

Detail

Sharpening

Amount	12
Radius	1.1
Detail	25
Masking	0

Noise Reduction

Luminance	14
Luminance Detail	42
Luminance Contrast	5
Color	6

7 Click on the **Open Image** button. This opens the image in Expert edit mode, from where it can also be saved as a standard file format such as JPEG

Open Image

The Sharpness of an image refers to the contrast between adjoining pixels, and can contribute to an image appearing more sharply in focus.

165

The Noise in an image refers to pixels that have not captured color accurately (mainly in low-level lighting) and can make images look "speckled". **Noise Reduction** in the RAW window can help reduce this, by dragging the available sliders.

Editing Multiple Images

The rise of digital cameras and smartphones with photographic capabilities means that we are now taking more photos than ever. In terms of editing, this can result in a lot of work if you want to perform similar or identical tasks on a number of images. However, in Elements there is an option for editing multiple files at the same time. This can be with a number of preset options, such as color quick fixes, renaming files and resizing files. To perform editing on multiple files:

 In Expert edit mode, select **File** > **Process Multiple Files** from the Menu bar

 The **Process Multiple Files** window contains all of the options for selecting and editing multiple files

The default file format for images taken with most digital cameras and smartphone cameras is JPEG (Joint Photographic Experts Group). However, this can be changed for a group of photos with the Process Multiple Files option.

Process Multiple Files

Learn more about: Process Multiple Files

Process Files From:	Folder ▼
Source:	
	Browse...
☐ Include All Subfolders	
Destination:	
	Browse...
☐ Same as Source	

File Naming
☐ Rename Files
Document Name ▼ + 3 Digit Serial Number ▼
Example: MyFile001.gif   Starting Serial #: 1
Compatibility: ☑ Windows ☐ Mac OS ☐ Unix

Image Size
☐ Resize Images
Width: ___ Centimeters ▼   Resolution: 150 ▼ dpi
Height: ___ Centimeters ▼
☑ Constrain Proportions

File Type
☐ Convert Files to: JPEG Max Quality ▼

☐ Log errors that result from processing files

Quick Fix
☐ Auto Levels
☐ Auto Contrast
☐ Auto Color
☐ Sharpen

Labels
Watermark ▼

Custom Text: ___

Position: Bottom Left ▼
Font: Tahoma ▼
T   12 ▼
Opacity: 50 ▼
Color: ■

Cancel   OK

Use the **Opened Files** option in Step 3 to perform a task on specific files, rather than on a whole folder.

 Click here to select options for the source location of the images to be edited. This can be

Process Files From:	Folder ▼
	Folder
Source:	Import
	Opened Files

either a folder, images imported from another location, or the currently-opened files

4 For the **Folder** option in Step 3, click on the **Browse...** button, navigate to the required folder and click on the **OK** button

Source:

Browse...

☐ Include All Subfolders
Destination:

☐ Same as Source

File Naming
☐ Rename Files

Document Name

Example: MyFile001.gif

Compatibility: ☑ Window

Image Size
☐ Resize Images

Width: [ ] Centim

Browse for Folder ✕

Choose a folder for processing multiple files...

∨ 🖿 Pictures
   2013-07
   2013-08
   2013-09
   2013-10
   2013-12
   2014-02
   2014-03
   2014-04
   2014-05
   2014-05-15

OK   Cancel

Beware

The more images in a folder, the longer it will take to process.

Beware

If you select the **Same as Source** option for the source of the processed files, these will overwrite the originals, even if the **Rename Files** option has been selected (it becomes deselected if Same as Source is selected).

5 Select a destination folder in the same way as for selecting the source folder

Source:

C:\Users\Nick\Pictures\2014-05-15\   Browse...

☐ Include All Subfolders
Destination:

C:\Users\Nick\Pictures\Processed\   Browse...

☐ Same as Source

6 Under the **Quick Fix** section, check on any of the fixes that you want applied to all of the images. The options are for **Auto Levels**, **Auto Contrast**, **Auto Color** and **Sharpen**

Quick Fix

☐ Auto Levels
☑ Auto Contrast
☑ Auto Color
☑ Sharpen

Hot tip

The Quick Fix options are a good way to edit a group of photos that have been taken under similar lighting conditions.

...cont'd

7 Under the **Image Size** section, check **On**

the **Resize Images** checkbox and enter the required dimensions and resolution. If **Constrain Proportions** is checked **On**, only one of the Width or Height boxes has to be completed, as the other one will be adjusted automatically, in proportion

Beware

PDF and TIFF file formats generally produce larger file sizes than JPEGs, which is a file format specifically designed to compress file size.

8 Check **On** the **Convert Files to:** button to select an option for converting the files into another file format; e.g. as PDFs or TIFFs

Don't forget

Once all of the required selections have been made for converting the files, click on the **OK** button.

9 Check **On** the **Rename Files** button to rename the batch of files based on a base document name and a sequential identifier

Applying Actions

Within Elements there are a number of preset editing actions that can be applied to images repeatedly, without having to perform all of the separate tasks individually. To do this:

1 In Expert edit mode, open the image to which you want to apply the action

2 Select **Window** > **Actions** from the Menu bar. Click here next to an Actions folder to expand it

3 Click on an action to select it

4 Click on this button to perform the action

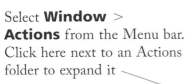

5 The action is performed and all of the required editing steps are applied to the image

The Actions panel does not have a keyboard shortcut.

You cannot create your own actions within Elements.

169

If you have the full version of Photoshop, you can import Actions from there. To do this, click on the Actions panel's menu (top, right corner) and select **Load Actions**. Navigate to the Actions folder within the Photoshop program files (**Presets** > **Actions**) and select an action there. Click on the **Load** button to add it.

Managing Catalogs

Elements manages your photos in catalogs, in which all of your photos are organized. By default, this is done in a single catalog, known as My Catalog. This can contain all of your photos and you can search for them using keywords, tags or by album. However, once you have thousands of photos covering dozens of subjects, this can start to get a little overwhelming. One option is to create new catalogs that can be used for specific subjects; e.g. one for travel and one for business. To create and manage different catalogs:

Don't forget

Catalogs cannot be accessed from any of the Editor modes.

Don't forget

The existence of catalogs does not change the physical locations of photos; they still remain in their original folders.

Hot tip

When a catalog is selected in Step 2, there is also an option to repair it. This can be done if images have been moved or deleted since the catalog was created.

1 In the Organizer, select **File** > **Manage Catalogs...** from the Menu bar

File | Edit | Find | View | He
 Get Photos and Video
 New
 Open Recently Edited
 Manage Catalogs...

2 The Catalog Manager dialog window displays the current catalog. Click here to select it and access options such as **Rename** or **Move**

Catalog Manager ✕

Elements Organizer keeps track of your media through a Catalog.

Most people keep all their media in one Catalog, which can have thousands of photos and videos. You might want a separate Catalog for a special purpose, such as business photos and videos. Each user of the program can have their own catalog.

New...
Convert...

Catalogs
⦿ Catalogs Accessible by All Users
○ Catalogs Accessible by the Current User
○ Custom Location

Browse...

My Catalog [Current]

Rename
Move
Remove
Optimize
Repair

Open   Cancel

3 Click on the **New...** button to create a new catalog

New...

4 Enter a name for the new catalog

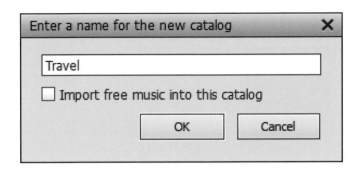

Enter a name for the new catalog   ✕

Travel

☐ Import free music into this catalog

    OK   Cancel

Don't forget

Make the names of catalogs as appropriate as possible to the intended subject matter.

5 Click on the **OK** button   OK

6 Click on the **Start Importing** button to add photos to the new catalog   Start Importing

Don't forget

Photos can be added to more than one catalog.

7 Check **On** the **Pictures** checkbox in the left-hand panel and click on individual folders in the main window to select or deselect them

Import Media   ✕

Import from following folders
Click on the folder to see its media on right panel.

1 subfolders selected from 1 folders

☑ Pictures

☑ 2015 10 19

☑ 2015 10 26

6 >

☑ 2015 10 27

Add Folder...   🗑 Remove   ⊘ Cancel   ➡ Import

Hot tip

Blank catalogs can be created by clicking on the **Cancel** button in the **Import Media** window in Step 7. Media can then be added to the new catalog from a camera or memory card, or a folder, using the **Import** option.

8 Click on the **Import** button to add selected folders

...cont'd

9 The photos are imported into the new catalog

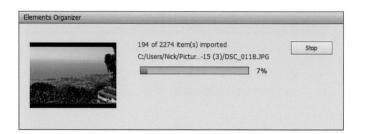

Hot tip

Click on the **Select All** or **Deselect All** buttons in Step 10 to select or deselect all of the keywords accordingly.

10 If keywords have been attached to any of the photos being imported, you will be able to include

the Keyword tags. Check **On** the checkboxes next to the required keywords and click on the **OK** button

11 Any photos that have been skipped for any reason, such as already being in the catalog, are detailed

Don't forget

If photos that are in an existing Elements catalog are imported into a new one, they will also remain in the original one.

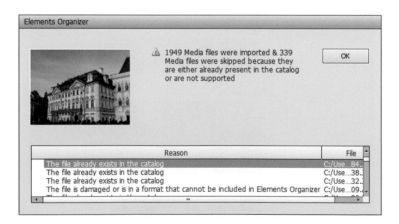

12 Click on the **OK** button

13 The new catalog is created and displayed within the Catalog Manager dialog window

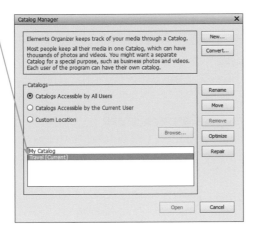

14 The photos in the new catalog are displayed in the same way as for the default catalog

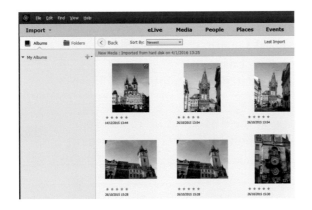

15 The name of the current catalog is displayed in the bottom right-hand corner of the Organizer window

Don't forget

New catalogs can be edited by selecting them in the **Catalog Manager** window and clicking on the **Rename**, **Move**, **Optimize** or **Repair** buttons.

Beware

Catalogs can be deleted by selecting them in the Catalog Manager and clicking on the **Remove** button. However, this can only be done when a catalog is not the one currently being viewed.

Hot tip

To change the catalog being viewed, select **File > Manage Catalogs** from the Organizer Menu bar. Select the required catalog in the **Catalog Manager** window and click on the **Open** button.

Viewing File Info

When digital images are taken, they create a considerable amount of related information, also known as metadata. To view this:

 Open an image in Expert or Quick edit mode

 Select **File** > **File Info** from the Menu bar

3 Click on the **Camera Data** button to view the information (metadata) that was created when the image was captured

`Camera Data`

4 The Camera Data information includes the **Camera Information**; i.e. the make and model of the camera, and the **Shot Information**; i.e. Focal Length, Exposure, Image Size, Orientation, Resolution and Flash

Camera Information

Make:	Canon
Model:	Canon EOS 350D DIGITAL; S/N: 2630703875
Owner:	
Lens:	

Shot Information

Focal Length:	21.00 mm
Exposure:	1/30 sec; f/4.0; ISO 800; Aperture priority; Pattern metering
Image Size:	3456 x 2304
Orientation:	1 (Normal)
Resolution:	72.00 Pixel per Inch
Flash:	Did not fire

5 Click on the **Basic** button to add your own additional metadata to the image

`Basic`

Document Title:	
Author:	
	Semicolons or commas can be used to separate multiple values
Author Title:	
Description:	
Rating:	☆ ☆ ☆ ☆ ☆
Description Writer:	
Keywords:	
	Semicolons or commas can be used to separate multiple values
Copyright Status:	Unknown
Copyright Notice:	
Copyright Info URL:	
Creation Date:	01/01/2018 11:26:02
Modification Date:	08/02/2018 13:44:27
Application:	Adobe Photoshop Elements 14.0 (Windows)

Don't forget

The **Shot Information** is created by the camera when a photo is taken.

Beware

Add a **Copyright Status** and a **Copyright Notice** in Step 5 if your photos are going to be published in public, and you are concerned that they may be used by others without your permission.

Save for Web

As digital cameras get more powerful in terms of the size and quality of images that they can capture, one issue is how to use these images on the web or in email: the larger the image, the longer it takes to send in an email or upload to the web. To overcome this, there is an option to save an image specifically for web use. To do this:

1 Open an image in Expert or Quick edit mode

2 Select **File > Save for Web** from the Menu bar to open the Save for Web window

3 The size of the original image is shown in the left-hand panel; the new size in the right-hand panel

The keyboard shortcut for the Save for Web dialog window is Alt + Shift + Ctrl + S (Alt + Shift + Command key + S on a Mac).

Next to the image size is an estimate for how long the image will take to download at different download speeds (which can be changed by clicking on the Menu button next to the current speed).

4 Click here to select a file format for the image for the web

GIF
GIF
JPEG
PNG-8
PNG-24

5 Enter a new size for the image to reduce the physical size of it; e.g. from 3024 x 3024 pixels to 500 x 500 pixels

New Size
Width: 3024 px
Height: 3024 px

New Size
Width: 500 px
Height: 500 px
Percent: 16.53 %

6 The size of the image in the right-hand panel is reduced accordingly (in this example, to 208K)

GIF
208.4K
39 sec @ 56.6 Kbps

Click on the **Save** button to exit the **Save for Web** window.

Save

Image Size

The physical size of a digital image can sometimes be a confusing issue, as it is frequently dealt with under the term "resolution". Unfortunately, resolution can be applied to a number of areas of digital imaging: image resolution, monitor resolution, print size and print resolution.

Image resolution

The resolution of an image is determined by the number of pixels it contains. This is counted as a vertical and a horizontal value; e.g. 4000 x 3000. When multiplied together it gives the overall resolution; i.e. 12,000,000 pixels in this case. This is frequently the headline figure quoted by camera manufacturers; e.g. 12 million pixels (or more commonly, 12 megapixels). To view the image resolution in Elements:

Hot tip

The keyboard shortcut for the Image Size dialog window is Alt + Ctrl + I (Alt + Command key + I on a Mac).

Hot tip

To view an image at its actual size, or the size at which it will currently be printed, select the **Zoom** tool from the Toolbox and select **1:1** or **Print Size** from the Tool Options bar.

1 Select **Image > Resize > Image Size** from the Menu bar

2 The image size is displayed here (in pixels)

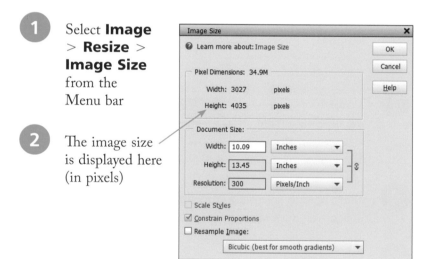

Don't forget

The Resolution figure under the Document Size heading is used to determine the size at which the image will be printed. If this is set to 96 pixels/inch, then the onscreen size and the printed size should be roughly the same.

Monitor resolution

Most modern computer monitors display digital images at between 72 and 96 pixels per inch (PPI). This means that every inch of the screen contains approximately this number of pixels. So, for an image being displayed at 100%, the onscreen size will be the number of pixels horizontally divided by 72 (or 96, depending on the monitor), and the same vertically. In the above example, this would mean the image, at actual size, could be viewed at approximately 31 inches by 42 inches (3027/96 and 4035/72) on a monitor. In modern web browsers, this is usually adjusted so that the whole image is accommodated on the viewable screen.

Document size (print resolution)

Pixels in an image are not a set size, which means that images can be printed in a variety of sizes, simply by contracting or expanding the available pixels. This is done by changing the resolution in the Document Size section of the Image Size dialog box. (When dealing with document size, think of this as the size of the printed document.) To set the size at which an image will be printed:

To work out the size at which an image will be printed, divide the pixel dimensions (height and width) by the resolution value under the Document Size heading.

1 Select **Image** > **Resize** > **Image Size** from the Menu bar

2 Change the resolution here (or change the width and height of the document size). Make sure the Resample Image box is not checked (see page 178)

Image Size	✕
❷ Learn more about: Image Size	OK
	Cancel
Pixel Dimensions: 34.9M	Help
Width: 3027 pixels	
Height: 4035 pixels	
Document Size:	
Width: 20.18 Inches ▼	
Height: 26.9 Inches ▼	
Resolution: 150 Pixels/Inch ▼	
☐ Scale Styles	
☑ Constrain Proportions	
☐ Resample Image:	
Bicubic (best for smooth gradients) ▼	

The print resolution determines how many pixels are used in each inch of the printed image (PPI). However, the number of dots used to represent each pixel on the paper is determined by the printer resolution, measured in dots per inch (DPI). So if the print resolution is 72 PPI and the printer resolution is 2880 DPI, each pixel will be represented by 40 colored dots; i.e. 2880 divided by 72.

3 By changing one value, the other two are updated too

Document Size:

Width:	15	Inches ▼
Height:	19.995	Inches ▼
Resolution:	201.8	Pixels/Inch ▼

4 Click on the **OK** button   OK

Resampling Images

All digital images can be increased or decreased in size. This involves adding or removing pixels from the image. Decreasing the size of an image is relatively straightforward and involves removing redundant pixels. However, increasing the size of an image involves adding pixels by digital guesswork. To do this, Elements looks at the existing pixels and works out the nearest match for the ones that are to be added. Increasing or decreasing the size of a digital image is known as "resampling".

Resampling

Resampling down decreases the size of the image, and it is more effective than resampling up. To do this:

The process of adding pixels to an image to increase its size is known as "interpolation".

To keep the same resolution for an image, resample it by changing the Pixel Dimensions' height and width.
To keep the same Document Size (i.e. the size at which it will be printed) resample it by changing the resolution.

1 Select **Image** > **Resize** > **Image Size** from the Menu bar

2 Check **On** the **Resample Image:** box

3 Resample the image by changing the pixel dimensions, the height and width, or the resolution

4 Changing any of the values in the Image Size dialog box alters the physical size of the image. Click on the **OK** button

Make sure the Constrain Proportions box is checked On if you want the image to be increased or decreased in size proportionally.

11 Printing Images

This chapter details sizing images and printing them in a variety of formats.

Print Size

Before you start printing images in Elements, it is important to ensure that they are going to be produced at the required size. Since the pixels within an image are not a set size, the printed dimensions of an image can be altered according to your needs. This is done by specifying how many pixels are used within each inch of the image. The more pixels per inch (PPI), then the higher the quality of the printed image, but the smaller in size it will be.

To set the print size of an image (in any of the Editor modes):

Don't forget

The higher the resolution in the Document Size section of the dialog, the greater the quality, but the smaller the size of the printed image.

1 Open an image and select **Image** > **Resize** > **Image Size** from the Menu bar

2 Uncheck the **Resample Image:** box. This will ensure that the physical image size (i.e. the number of pixels in the image) remains unchanged when the resolution is changed

Hot tip

The output size for a printed image can be worked out by dividing the pixel dimensions (the width and height) by the resolution. So if the width is 2560, the height 1920, and the resolution 300 PPI, the printed image will be approximately 8 inches by 6 inches.

Image Size ✕

❓ Learn more about: Image Size

OK
Cancel
Help

Pixel Dimensions: 34.9M

Width: 3024 pixels
Height: 4032 pixels

Document Size:

Width: 51.21 Centimeters ▾
Height: 68.28 Centimeters ▾
Resolution: 150 Pixels/Inch ▾

☐ Scale Styles
☑ Constrain Proportions
☐ Resample Image:

Bicubic (best for smooth gradients) ▾

Don't forget

As long as the Resample Image box is unchecked, changing the output resolution has no effect on the actual number of pixels in an image.

 3 The current resolution and document size (print size) are displayed here

4 Enter a new figure in the **Resolution:** box (here, the resolution has been increased from 150 to 300). This affects the document size; i.e. the size at which the image prints

Viewing print size

In Expert edit mode, images can be viewed at their print size:

1 Click on the Zoom tool

2 In the Tool Options, click on the **Print Size** button

3 The image is displayed at the size at which it will be printed. Change the resolution to see how this changes the print size

181

Print Functions

The Print functions in Elements can be accessed from the Menu bar in either the Editor or the Organizer, by selecting **File > Print**. Also, all of the print functions can be selected from Create mode. To print to your local printer using this method:

Hot tip

The keyboard shortcut for printing images is Ctrl + P, in either Editor or Organizer mode (Command key + P on a Mac).

Don't forget

The currently-active images are shown in the left-hand panel of the Print window.

Hot tip

Check **On** the **Crop to Fit** checkbox to crop the photo to ensure it fits on the page. Check the photo to ensure that it still appears as required.

1 Select an image in either the Editor or the Organizer, click on the **Create** button and click on the **Photo Prints** button

2 Click on the **Local Printer** button

3 The main print window displays the default options for how the printed image will appear, and also options for changing the properties of the print

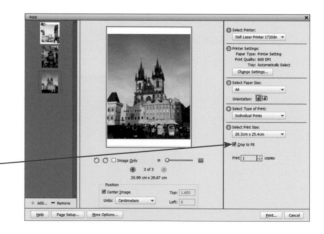

4 Click the **Add...** button to include more images in the current print job, or select an image and click on the **Remove** button to exclude it

5 Use these options to rotate an image for printing, or change its size or position

> ↺ ↻ ☐ Image Only
>
> ◀ **2 of 2** ▶
>
> 29.67 cm x 20.99 cm
>
> **Position**
> ☑ Center Image   Top: 1.693
> Units: cm ▼   Left: 1.658

Hot tip

Check on the **Center Image** box in Step 5 to have the image printed in the center of the page.

6 Click here to select a destination printer to which you want to send your print

> **1** Select Printer:
>
> Dell Laser Printer 1720dn (C... ▼

7 Click on the **Change Settings...** button to change the properties for your own local printer

> **2** Printer Settings:
>   Paper Type: Printer Setting
>   Print Quality: 600 DPI
>   Tray: Automatically Select
>
> Change Settings...

8 Click here to select the paper size for printing

> **3** Select Paper Size:
>
> A4 ▼
>
> Orientation: 🔲 🔲

Don't forget

The other options for Type of Print in Step 9 are **Picture Package** and **Contact Sheet**. See pages 184-185 for more details.

9 Click here to select the print type; i.e. the layout of the image you are printing

> **4** Select Type of Print:
>
> Individual Prints ▼

10 Click here to select the size at which you want your image to be printed

> **5** Select Print Size:
>
> Actual Size (25.47cm x 16.9... ▼
>
> ☐ Crop to Fit

11 Click on the **Print...** button to print your image with the settings selected above

> Print...

Print Layouts

Rather than just offering the sole function of printing a single image on a sheet of paper, Elements has two options that can be used when printing images, which can help reduce the number of sheets of paper used.

Picture Package

This can be used to print out copies of different images on a single piece of paper. To do this:

Hot tip

When buying a printer, choose one that has borderless printing. This means that it can print to the very edge of the page.

1 Select an image in either the Editor or the Organizer, click on the Create button, and then click on the **Picture Package** button

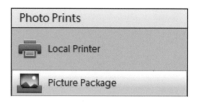

Don't forget

The Picture Package option is also available if you print photos using **File** > **Print** (or Ctrl + P; Command + P on a Mac) from the Menu bar. In the **Prints** dialog window, select **Picture Package** under the **Select Type of Print:** heading.

2 The layout for the Picture Package is displayed in the main print window

Don't forget

The Picture Package function is useful for printing images in a combination of sizes, such as for family portraits.

3 Under **Select a Layout:**, select how many images you want on a page and if required, select a type of frame for the printed images

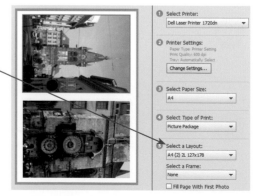

Contact Sheet

This can be used to create and print thumbnail versions of a large number of images. To do this:

 1 Select an image in either the Editor or the Organizer, click on the Create button and then click on the **Contact Sheet** button

2 The layout for the Contact Sheet is displayed in the main Print window

When a Contact Sheet is created, new thumbnail images are generated. The original images are unaffected.

Do not include too many thumbnails on a Contact Sheet, otherwise they may be too small to see any detail clearly.

3 Click under **Select Type of Print:** and select the number of columns to be displayed on the Contact Sheet

4 Select Type of Print:

Contact Sheet ▼

☑ Crop to Fit

Select a Layout:
Columns: 4 ↕ (1-9)

Creating PDF Files

PDF (Portable Document Format) is a file format that is used to maintain the original formatting and style of a document, so that it can be viewed on a variety of different devices and types of computers. In general, it is usually used for documents that contain text and images, such as information pamphlets, magazine features, and chapters from books. However, image files such as JPEGs can also be converted into PDFs, and this can be done within Elements without the need for any other specialist software. To do this:

PDF files are an excellent way to share files so that other people can print them. All that is required is a copy of Adobe Acrobat Reader, which is bundled with most software packages on computers, or can be downloaded from the Adobe website at **www.adobe.com**

PDF files are generally larger in terms of file size than standard image file formats such as JPEG.

 Open an image and select **File** > **Save As** from the Menu bar

 Select a destination folder and make sure the format is set to Photoshop PDF, then click **Save**

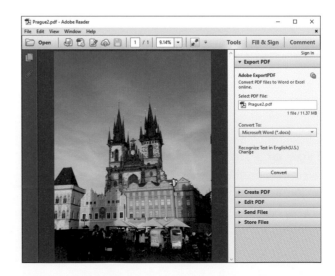

The PDF file is created and can be opened in Adobe Acrobat or Elements

Index

P